William Dean Howells, Mark Twain

The Niagara book

A Complete Souvenir of Niagara Falls, Containing Sketches, Stories and Essays ...

William Dean Howells, Mark Twain

The Niagara book
A Complete Souvenir of Niagara Falls, Containing Sketches, Stories and Essays ...

ISBN/EAN: 9783743442016

Manufactured in Europe, USA, Canada, Australia, Japa

Cover: Foto ©Andreas Hilbeck / pixelio.de

Manufactured and distributed by brebook publishing software (www.brebook.com)

William Dean Howells, Mark Twain

The Niagara book

The American Rapids by Moonlight.

THE NIAGARA BOOK

A COMPLETE SOUVENIR OF NIAGARA FALLS

CONTAINING SKETCHES, STORIES AND ESSAYS—DESCRIPTIVE, HUMOROUS, HISTORICAL AND SCIENTIFIC,

WRITTEN EXCLUSIVELY FOR THIS BOOK.

BY

W. D. HOWELLS, MARK TWAIN,
PROF. NATHANIEL S. SHALER, AND OTHERS.

FULLY ILLUSTRATED BY HARRY FENN

BUFFALO
UNDERHILL AND NICHOLS
1893

THE WENBORNE-SUMNER CO. PRESS,
BUFFALO, N. Y.

Preface.

The lack of a good souvenir of Niagara Falls has often been noted by visitors at the great cataract. The editors and publishers of this volume have endeavored, by securing the co-operation of the most prominent literary men in America, to supply such a need. By following an idea of their own they have persuaded representative men in their lines to write for the book original stories, sketches and essays—descriptive, humorous, historical and scientific — dealing directly with Niagara Falls. One of the greatest artists in the country has prepared the water-color sketches and the novel drawings from which the illustration plates are made, and the publishers confidently trust that the entire volume will appeal to all the world by reason of its completeness. That this is America's greatest anniversary year lends special relevance to the publication of such a book.

BUFFALO, N. Y , June 1, 1893.

CONTENTS.

	PAGE
PREFACE	
NIAGARA, FIRST AND LAST BY W. D. HOWELLS.	1
WHAT TO SEE BY FREDERIC ALMY.	28
THE GEOLOGY OF NIAGARA FALLS BY PROF. N. S. SHALER.	65
THE FIRST AUTHENTIC MENTION OF NIAGARA FALLS BY MARK TWAIN.	93
FAMOUS VISITORS AT NIAGARA FALLS BY THOMAS R. SLICER.	110
HISTORIC NIAGARA BY PETER A. PORTER.	140
THE FLORA AND FAUNA OF NIAGARA FALLS BY DAVID F. DAY.	170
AS IT RUSHES BY BY EDWARD S. MARTIN.	186
THE UTILIZATION OF NIAGARA'S POWER BY COLEMAN SELLERS, E. D.	193
THE HYDRAULIC CANAL BY W. C. JOHNSON.	221

ILLUSTRATIONS.

THE AMERICAN RAPIDS BY MOONLIGHT - -	Frontispiece.
	SEE PAGE
A BIT OF THE AMERICAN FALLS FROM BELOW THE CAVE OF THE WINDS—SUMMER -	16
A BIT OF THE AMERICAN FALLS FROM BELOW THE CAVE OF THE WINDS—WINTER. - -	34
THE HORSE SHOE FALLS FROM THE THREE SISTERS—THE DUFFERIN ISLANDS IN THE DISTANCE. - - - - - - -	46
A BIRD'S-EYE VIEW OF NIAGARA RIVER -	64
A MAP OF THE HYDROGRAPHY AT A DATE BEFORE THE MELTING OF THE GREAT GLACIER - - - - - - -	70
A MAP OF THE HYDROGRAPHY AT A DATE AFTER THE MELTING OF THE GREAT GLACIER - - - - - - -	74
A MAP OF LAKE IROQUOIS - - - -	77
NIAGARA FALLS, SHOWING THE HARD AND SOFT STRATA - - - - - -	83
A BIRD'S-EYE VIEW OF THE NIAGARA RIVER GORGE - - - - - - -	88

(The six illustrations on pages 64, 70, 74, 77, 83, 88 are reprinted from Gilbert's report of the New York State Reservation).

The Horse Shoe Falls from Goat Island	SEE PAGE 98
The Whirlpool Rapids with the Cantilever Bridge above	128
A Map of the Niagara River—Showing Points of Historic Interest	154
Niagara Falls—From an Old Drawing by Father Hennepin	169
Looking Towards the Three Sisters from Canada	174
The Inlet Canal and Niagara River	197
The Interior of the Tunnel	202
Transverse Sketch, Showing Inlet from Main Canal	206
The Discharge Portal	215

The half-tone illustrations and decorative headings for all the articles are reproduced from original sketches by Harry Fenn.

NIAGARA: FIRST & LAST

By WILLIAM D. HOWELLS

I

IN the spring of 1860 I wrote a life of Lincoln. It was what is called a campaign life, and in its poor way it was a part of the electioneering enginery of a canvass destined to be, if not the most memorable in our history, at least of the farthest effect. To be quite honest, I must own that my book, as I now look back on the facts, probably served the mysterious uses, and performed the vague offices of a fifth wheel to a coach, in forwarding the fortunes of the man whose life it celebrated before he was so famous as to need no blare of trumpets, not to say willow whistles, evermore. What seems strange is that the great renown of Lincoln has not reacted upon one of his earliest biographies; that this has dropped as wholly in oblivion as if it was the story of nobody; the coach indeed arrived in glory, and was found to be the car of victory, the fiery chariot of freedom; but the fifth wheel seems to have stopped somewhere on the way.

My book was published in Columbus, Ohio, and I did not wait for its assured success before setting forth upon some travels which had long invited me. The publisher had so much faith in it as to be willing to supply me in advance with a certain sum of money, say fifty dollars in Ohio money, and a letter of credit, addressed to several publishers in Boston and New York, to the amount of some hundred and ninety dollars more. I meant to explore those distant capitals, and to take in the wonders and delights of the St. Lawrence route to Quebec, and to acquaint myself with the manners and customs of strange peoples, so far as they were to be studied in Canada. For this journey, a great deal of money was needed, and I took all I had. I do not know why I should have thought it well to spend my whole substance upon this venture, but I seem to have done so; and I had no compunctions, so far as I can remember, in spending so much of this vast sum in Ohio money, which I then believed the best money in the world. I found later that it was worth only eighty-five or ninety cents on the dollar in Boston; one was liable to these surprises in the days of State banking; but as yet I was troubled with no misgivings when I left Columbus, and took my way to Buffalo, where I thought I might fitly rest a day or two, and recruit my strength for the impression of Niagara which I was eager to receive. I spent most of this stay in my room at the hotel, writing letters for a

Cincinnati paper, which had agreed to take them from me. The passion for summer correspondence has not yet died out of journalism, but even then I found its impulses uncertain, and many of the letters I wrote on that journey were never printed. I am not sure that this was a loss to literature; but it certainly was a loss to me in that Ohio money which was the best in the world. When I was not writing, I was wandering about the streets of Buffalo, and viewing its monuments from the platform of a horse car, or from its pavements, not so much crowded then as now. I forget what the monuments were in that day; I even forget who were the editors of the papers, whom I visited after the simple journalistic usage of the time, and conversed with, in their offices. But they probably had their revenge, and forgot who I was much sooner. I recall, however, that it was all very stirring and interesting, and that I tried to view the novelties I found everywhere in the manner of my favorite authors, and to describe them in their style. The chief of these authors was then Heinrich Heine, and I did my best to give such an account of Buffalo as he would have written in English if he had been there in my place. As soon as I had completed the history of my observations, which was more considerable than the observations themselves, I pushed on to Niagara Falls.

II.

One always experiences a vivid emotion from the sight of the Rapids, no matter how often one sees them, but I am safe in saying that one sees them for the first time but once. After that one has the feeling of a habitué towards them, a sort of friendly and familiar appreciation of their terrific beauty, but certainly not the thrill of the pristine awe. It is even hard to recall that: the picture remains, but not the sense of their mighty march, or of their gigantic leaps and lunges, when they break ranks, and their procession becomes a mere onward tumult without form or order. I had schooled myself for great impressions, and I did not mean to lose one of them; they were all going into that correspondence which I was so proud to be writing, and finally, I hoped, they were going into literature: poems, sketches, studies, and I do not know what all. But I had not counted upon the Rapids taking me by the throat, as it were, and making my heart stop. I still think that above and below the Falls, the Rapids are the most striking features of the spectacle. At least you may say something about them, compare them to something; when you come to the cataract itself, you can say nothing; it is incomparable. My sense of it first, and my sense of it last, was not a sense of the stupendous, but a sense of beauty, of serenity, of repose. I have always had to take myself in hand, to shake myself up, to look twice, and recur to what I have heard and read of other people's impressions, before I am overpowered by it. Otherwise I am simply charmed.

I hurried out to look at it as soon as they gave me a room in the good old Cataract House, and I spent the afternoon in taking a careful account of my impressions, and trying to fit phrases to my emotions for that blessed correspondence. Then I went back to my room and began to put them down on paper while they were still warm.

That pleasant room in the Cataract House is very vivid in my memory yet. It had a green lattice-door opening into the corridor, and when I left the inner door ajar, a delicious current of summer breeze and afternoon sunshine drew through it from the window looking out on a sweep of those Rapids. It was what they call a single room, but it seemed very spacious at that time, and it had a little table in it, where I wrote my letters to the Cincinnati paper. I lived two weeks in that room, and I made a vast deal of copy, including some poems, I believe, which never got printed, any more than most of my letters, though I did not confine the test of their merit to one editor alone.

III.

Apart from these literary enterprises of mine there was not a great deal to occupy me in the hotel. I suppose there are moments when the hotels at Niagara are full, but I never happened there at those moments, and the Cataract House at the time of my first visit was far from crowded, though it was in the days before the war when Southerners were reputed to visit the Falls in great numbers. We dined at mid-day to the music of a brass band, which must have been more than usually brazen, to have affected my nerves the way it did, for at twenty-three the nerves are not sensitive. Very likely there were a variety of brides and grooms there, but I did not know them from the rest: so little is one condition of life able to distinguish another. There was a period when these young couples were visible to me, afterwards; and then, when I was very much older, they vanished again, and were no more to be found by the eye of earlier age than by the eye of earlier youth. I believe I saw numbers of pretty young girls, who then appeared to me stately and mature women, of great splendor and beauty, and of varying measures of haughty inapproachability. I made the acquaintance of no one in the hotel, but by a sort of affinition, which I should now be at a loss to account for, I fell in with two artists who were painting the Falls and the Rapids, and the scenery generally, and I used to go about with them, and watch them at their work. They were brothers, and very friendly fellows, not much older than I, and because I liked them, and was reaching out in every direction for the materials of greater and greater consciousness, I tried to see Niagara as actively and pervasively iridescent as they did. They invited me to criticise their pictures in the presence of the facts, and I did once intimate that I failed to find all those rainbows, of different sizes and shapes which they had represented on the surface of the water everywhere. Then they pointed the rainbows out with their forefingers and asked, Didn't I see them there, and there, and there? I looked very hard, and as I was not going to be outdone in the perception of beauty, I said that I did see them, and I tried to believe that I saw them, but Heaven knows I never did. I hope this fraud will not be finally accounted against me. Those were charming fellows, and other pictures of theirs I have found so faithful that I am still a little shaken about the rainbows. My artists were from Ohio, and though I was too ignorant then to affirm that Ohio art was the best art in the world, just as Ohio money was the best, still I was very proud of it, and I suppose I renowned those invisible iridescences in my letter to the Cincinnati paper.

We walked all about the Falls, and over Goat Island, and to and from the Whirlpool, and it was a great advantage to me to be in the artists' company, for they knew all the loveliest places, and could show me the best points of view. I drove nowhere, because I had a fear, bred of much newspaper rumor and humor, that my accumulated treasures would not hold out against the rapacity of a single Niagara hackman. A dollar was a dollar in those days, especially if it were a dollar of Ohio money, or at least it was so till you got to Boston; and I was not willing to waste any of mine in carriage fares. But to be honest about those poor fellows, I always found the Niagara hackmen, when I visited their domain in after years, not only civil but reasonable, and I have never regretted the money I spent upon them; it was no longer Ohio money, to be sure.

Some places I could not walk to on that first visit, and as there was no suspension bridge then near the Falls, I took a boat when I wished to cross to the Canada side, and a man rowed me over the eddies of the river where they reeled away from the plunge of the cataract. I do not think I crossed more than once, or had any wish to do so, after I had visited the battle field of Lundy's Lane, where a veteran of the fight, so well preserved in alcohol that I should not be surprised if he were there yet, gave me an account of it from the top of a tower in which he seemed to be fortified. That poor little carnage has shrunken into so small a horror since the battles of the great war, then impending, that I feel somewhat like excusing the mention of it now; but when I visited the scene in 1860, I was aware of several emotions which, if not of prime importance on the spot, were very capable of being worked up into something worth while in my letter to the Cincinnati paper. I tried to give them a

Heinesque cast, and I made a good deal of the tipsy veteran. In the course of a literary life one is obliged to practice these economies, and I advise the beginner in our art against throwing away anything whatever. But what is the need of advising him? He would not be able to do so if he wished. He belongs to what he has seen, as much as it belongs to him, and he owes it a debt of expression which will weigh upon him till he complies with its just demand. The trouble is with what he has not seen, and decidedly he had better not be advised against throwing that away. The more of that he throws away the better; and the reader can have very little notion how much he is profiting by my profusion in this respect.

IV.

Really, however, I did see a great many things at Niagara on that first visit, and I am sorry to say that I saw them chiefly on the Canada side. My patriotism has always felt the hurt of the fact that our great national cataract is best viewed from a foreign shore. There can be no denying, at least in a confidence like the present, that the Canadian Fall, if not more majestic is certainly more massive, than the American. I used to watch its mighty wall of waters with a jealousy almost as green as themselves, and then try to believe that the knotted tumble of our Fall was finer. I could only make out that it had more apparent movement.

But at times, and if one looked steadily at any part of the cataract, the descending floods seemed to hang in arrest above the gulfs below. Those liquid steeps, those precipices of molten emerald, all broken and fissured with opal and crystal, seemed like heights of sure and firmset earth, and the mists that climbed them half-way were as still to the eye in their subtler sort. This effect of immobility is what gives its supreme beauty to Niagara, its repose. If there is agony there, it is the agony of Niobe, of the Laocoon. It moves the beholder, but itself it does not move.

I spent a great deal of time trying to say this or something like it, which now and always seemed to me true of Niagara, though I do not insist that it shall seem so to others. I could not see those iridescences that everywhere illumined the waters to my artist friends, and very likely the reader, if he is a person of feeble fancy, small sympathy and indifferent morals, will find nothing of this Repose that I speak of in Niagara. I imagine him taking my page out into the presence of the fact, and demanding, Now where is the Repose?

Well, all that I can say is that it has always been there on the occasion of my visits. On the occasion of my first visit there was even a shelf of the Table Rock still there, and I went out and stood upon it, for the sake of saying that I had done so in my letter to the Cincinnati paper, though I might very well have said it without having done so, and I am almost sorry that I did not, when I remember how few of those letters that paper printed. There was no great pleasure in the experience. You were supposed to get a particularly fine view of the Horseshoe Falls, but I got no view at all, on account of a whim of the mist. Weeks earlier a large piece of the rock had fallen just a few moments after a carriage full of people had driven off it, and I did not know but another piece might fall just a few moments before I walked off it. I was not in a carriage, and my portion of Table Rock did not fall till some three months later; that was quite soon enough for me; I should have preferred three years.

I do not know whether it was my satisfaction in this hair-breadth escape or not, but I had sufficient spirits immediately after to join a group of people near by who were taking peeps over a precipice at something below. I did not know what it was, but I thought it might be something I could work up in my letters to that Cincinnati paper, and I waited my turn among those who were lying successively on their stomachs and craning their necks over the edge; and then I saw that it was a man who was lying face upwards on the rocks below, and had perhaps been lying there some time. He was a very green and yellow melancholy of a man, as to his face, and in his workman's blue overalls he had a trick of swimming upwards to the eye of the æsthetic spectator, so that one had to push back with a hard clutch on the turf to keep from plunging over to meet him. I made a note of this morbid impulse for primary use in my letters to that Cincinnati paper, and secondary use in a poem, or sketch, or tale; and then I crawled back and went away, and was faint in secret for a while. It was strange how fully sufficing one little glimpse of that poor man was. No one knew who he was or how he had fallen over there, but after the first glance at him (I believe I did not give a second) I felt that we did not part strangers. Now I meet people at dinner and pass whole evenings with them, and cannot remember their faces so as to place them the next week. But I think I could have placed that poor man years afterwards. To be sure the circumstances are different, and I am no longer twenty-three.

V.

Do they still, I wonder, take people to see a place not far above the Canadian Fall, where a vein of natural gas vents itself amid the trouble of the waters, and the custodian sets fire to it with a piece of lighted newspaper? They used to do that, if you paid them a quarter, in a little pavilion built over the place to shut out the unpaying public. By comparison with the great gas wells which I saw in combustion long after at Findlay, this was a very feeble rush light conflagration indeed, but it had the merit of being much more mysterious. I, for instance, did not know it was natural gas, or what it was, and the custodian sagely would not say; the mystery was probably part of his stock in trade. There were many mysteries, maintained at a profit, about Niagara then, and not the least of them was the Terrapin Tower, which stood at the brink of the American Fall, and was reached by a series of stepping stones and bridges amidst the rapids. The mystery of this was that any human being should wish to go up it, at the risk of his life, but everybody did. I myself found a bridal couple (of the third espousals) in it when I ventured a vast deal of potential literature in its frail keeping; no terrapin, I fancy, was ever so rash as to ascend it, from the day it was built to the day it was taken away. What is so amusing now to think of, though not so amusing then, is that all the while I was clambering about those heights and brinks, I was suffering from an inveterate vertigo, which made plain ground rather difficult for me at times. At odd moments it became necessary for me to lay hold of something and stay the reeling world; and the recurrence of these exigences finally decided me against venturing into the Cave of the Winds. Upon the whole I am glad I did not penetrate it, for now I can think it what I like, and if I had seen it I probably could not do that. I compromised by descending the Biddle Stairs, which had a rail to hold on by, and which, I have no doubt, amount to much the same thing as the

Cave of the Winds. At any rate, when I got to the bottom of them, I wondered why in the world I had come down.

I do not know whether under the present socialistic regime, or state control, of the Falls, there are so many marvels shown as under the old system of private enterprise. But I am sure that their number could have been greatly reduced, with advantage to the visitor. If you find a marvel advertised, and you learn that you cannot see it without paying a quarter, every coin upon your person begins to burn in an intense sympathy with your curiosity, and you cannot be content till you have seen that marvel. This was the principle of human nature upon which private capital had counted, and it did not matter that the Falls themselves were enough to glut the utmost greed of wonder. Their prodigious character was eked out by every factitious device to which the penalty of twenty-five cents could be attached. I remember that at the entrance of Prospect Park, if not within the sacred grove, a hardy adventurer had pitched his tent and announced the presence of a five-legged calf within its canvas walls, in active competition with the great cataract. I paid my quarter (my Ohio money was all paper, or I might have thought twice about it,) in order to make sure that this calf was in no wise comparable to Niagara. I do not say that the picture of the calf on the outside of the tent was not as good as some pictures of Niagara that I have seen. It was at least as much like.

I hope that all this is not decrying the attractions of any worthy adjunct of the cataract, such as the Whirlpool. There is of course no other such, and I was proud and glad to believe that the Whirlpool was chiefly on the American side, or the first part of it, or was at first nearly if not solely accessible from our territory; and I did not find out till long after that I was wrong. The Whirlpool, seen from the heights around it, has that effect of sculpturesque repose which I have always found the finest thing in the Cataract itself. Like that it is impassioned, while the Rapids are passionate. From the top the circling lines of the Whirlpool seemed graven in a level of chalcedony; the illusion of arrest was so perfect that I was almost sorry ever to have lost it, though I do not know what I could have done with it if I had kept it. I duly studied my phrases about it for my letters to that Cincinnati paper, and it is probably from some of them, printed or unprinted, that I speak now. These things linger long in the mind; and it is not always from frugality that the observer of the picturesque uses the same terms again and again. Happily, I am not obliged to describe the Whirlpool to the reader, as I was then, and I have no impression to impart except this sense of its worthy unity with the Cataract in what I may call its highest æsthetic quality, its repose.

VI.

If he does not believe in this, he may go and look; but there is one fact of this first visit of mine to Niagara which he must helplessly take my word for. That fact is Blondin, who is closely allied in my mind with the Whirlpool, because I saw him cross the river above the frantic Rapids not far from it. If this association is too mechanical, too material, then I will go farther, and say that when Blondin had got such a distance into the danger, he, too, became an illusion of Repose; and I defy the most skeptical reader, who was not then present, to gainsay me.

Why those rapids just below the large Suspension Bridge were chosen to stretch Blondin's cable over, I do not know, unless it was because the river narrows to a gorge there, and because those rapids are more horrid, in the eighteenth-century sense, than any other feature of Niagara. They have been a great deal exploited since Blondin's time by adventurers who have attempted to swim them, and to navigate them in barrels and buoys and India-rubber balls, or if not quite India-rubber balls, I do not know why. But at that time no craft but the Maid-of-the-Mist, the little steamboat which used to run up to the foot of the cataract, had ever dared them. She, indeed, flying from the perennial pun involved in her name, not to mention the Sheriff's officer who had an attachment for her, weathered the rapids and passed in and out of the

A bit of American Falls from below the Cave of the Winds—Summer

Whirlpool, and escaped into the quiet of Canadian waters, with the pilot and her engineer on board. Afterwards I saw her at Quebec where she had changed her name, as other American refugees in Canada have done, and had now become the Maid-of-Orleans, in recognition of her peaceful employ of carrying people to and from the Isle of Orleans. But her adventurous voyage was still fresh on the lips of guides and hackmen when I was first at Niagara, and I looked at the Rapids and the Whirlpool with an interest peculiarly fearful because of it.

As usual, I walked to the scene of the exploit I was about to witness, but there were a good many people walking, and they debated on the way whether Blondin would cross that day or not. It had been raining over night, and some said his cable was not in condition; others, that the guys which stayed it on either side were too slack, or too taut from the wet. Nevertheless, we found a great crowd on the Canada shore, which seemed to command the best view of Blondin as well as Niagara, and the American shore was dense with spectators, too. As the hour drew near for Blondin to do his feat, we were lost in greater and greater doubt whether he would do it or not, and perhaps if a vote had been taken the skeptics would have carried the day, when he suddenly danced out upon the cable before our unbelieving eyes.

The dizzy path was of the bigness of a ship's cable,

at the shore, but it seemed to dwindle to a thread where it sank over the centre of the gulf, down toward those tusked and frothing breakers. They seemed to jump at it, like a pack of maddened wolves, and to pull one another back, and then to tumble and flow away, forever different, forever the same. The strong guys starting from the rocks of the precipice and the level of the rapids could stay it, after all, only a little part of its length, and beneath them and up through them, the black cedars thrust their speary tops, with that slant toward the middle of the gorge, which must be from the pull of the strong draft between its walls. They made a fine contrast of color with the floods breaking snowy white from their bulks of glassy green; and for the rest there was the perfect blue of the summer heaven over all.

There was no testing of the guys, whether they were slack or taut, or of the cable, whether it was in condition, and in fact no one thought of either, such was the surprise of seeing that pink figure of a man spring out into space from some source which I, at least, had not observed. He was in the conventional silk fleshings of the rope-dancer, and he carried a very long balancing pole. At first there was some reality in the apparition. One felt he was a fellow-man about to dare death for our amusement, but as he began to run down the slope of the cable toward the centre, one rapidly lost this sense, and beheld him as a mere feature of the general prospect. Perhaps he was aware of this effect and chose to startle us back to our consciousness of his humanity, or perhaps it was a wonted trick, intended to heighten the interest of the spectacle. At any rate, in the very middle of the river, he seemed suddenly to falter, and he swayed from side to side as if he were going to fall. A sort of groan went through the crowd, and several women fainted. Then Blondin made believe to recover himself, and began to climb the slope of his cable to the further shore. I do not know just how far this was, but I think it may have been well on to half a mile; as to the height above the rapids where the cable hung it looked like a hundred and fifty feet. I made some vague note of these matters after Blondin vanished into the crowd beyond, but there was not much time for conjecture. He came into sight again almost at once, a little puppet, running down the farther slope of the cable, and growing a little and a little larger as he drew near. Presently one noticed that he had left his balancing pole behind, and was tripping forward with outstretched arms.

I stood where I could see him well, on his return, and I looked at him with something of the interest one might feel in a man who had come back from the dead and had put on his earthly personality again. I do not remember his face, which was no doubt as good or as bad a face as any mountebank's or monarch's, but his feet seemed to me the very most intelligent feet in the world, pliable, sinuous, clinging, educated in every fibre, and full of spiritual sentience. They had the air of knowing that the whole man was trusted to them, and, such as he was, that he was in their power and keeping alone. They rose and fell upon the cable with an exquisite accuracy, and a delicate confidence which had nothing foolhardy in it. Blondin's head might take risks, but it was clear that Blondin's feet took none; whatever they did they did wittingly, and with a full forecast of the chances and consequences. They were imaginably such feet as Isaac Taylor conjectures we may have in another life, where the intellect shall not be seated in the brain alone, but shall be issued to every part of the body, and present in every joint and limb.

They were an immense consolation to me, those feet, and when Blondin went tripping gayly out upon them over his rope again, I breathed much more freely than I had before; they had, as it were, personally reassured me, and given me their honor that nothing should happen to him; those feet and I had a sort of common understanding about him, and I do not think they respected him any more than I did for risking his life in that manner. He went down the rope and up the rope, dwindling from a pink man to a pink puppet as before, and going to nothing in the crowd. Then he came to something once more, and began to grow from a puppet into a man again, but with something odd about him. He had resumed his balancing pole, and he had something strange on his feet, those wise feet, and, as he drew nearer, we could see that he had wooden buckets on them, of about the bigness of butter firkins; I tell it, not expecting much to be believed, for I did not believe it when I saw it. But till he arrived, I could say to myself that there were no bottoms in those buckets, and that his sagacious feet, though somewhat impeded, had still no doubt a good chance to save him, if he lost his head, and would be equal to any common emergency. That was the opinion of everyone about me, and though I knew how vexed with him the feet must be, I did not wholly lose patience till I was told by one who saw the buckets after Blondin stepped out of them, that they had wooden bottoms like any other butter firkins. Then I was glad that I did not see his feet again, for I could imagine the look of cold disgust, the look of haughty injury they must wear at having been made privy to such a mere brutal audacity

The man himself looked cool and fresh enough, but I, who was not used to such violent fatigues as he must have undergone in these three transits, was bathed in a cold perspiration, and so weak and worn with making them in sympathy that I could scarcely walk away.

Long afterwards I was telling about this experience of mine—it was really more mine than Blondin's—in the neat shop of a Venetian pharmacist, to a select circle of the physicians who wait in such places in Venice for the call of their patients. One of these civilized men, for all comment, asked: "Where was the government?" and I answered in my barbarous pride of our individualism, "The government had nothing to do with it. In America the government has nothing to do with such things."

But now I think that this Venetian was right, and that such a show as I have tried to describe, ought no more to have been permitted than the fight of a man with a wild beast. It was an offence to morality, and it thinned the frail barrier which the aspiration of centuries has slowly erected between humanity and savagery. But for the time being I made no such reflections. I got back to my hotel and hastened to send off a whole letter about Blondin to that Cincinnati paper; and to this day I do not know whether they ever printed it or not. I try to make fun of it now, but it was not funny then. All the way round on that tour, my view of the wonders of nature and the monuments of man was obscured by my anxiety concerning the letters I wrote to that Cincinnati paper; and at all the hotels where I stopped I hurried to examine the files of the reading-room and see whether it had kept faith with me or not. Across many years, across graves not a few, I can reach and recall the hurt vanity, the just resentment, and the baffled hope, that were bound up in that early experience of editorial frailty.

VII.

My first visit to Niagara was paid in the midsummer of the year, and the midsummer of my life. All nature was rich and beautifully alive amid scenes which I think are of her noblest. There were places where the fresh scent of the waters was mixed with the fragrance of wild flowers; the birds which sang inaudibly in the immediate roar of the cataract, made themselves sweetly heard in the heart of Goat Island. Everywhere there were pretty young girls, in the hats which they were then beginning to wear after a long regime of bonnets, and their hats had black plumes in them that drooped down as near to the cheeks of the pretty young girls as they could get.

I can scarcely help heaving a sigh for the wrinkles in those cheeks which the plumes, if they still drooped instead of sticking militantly up on the front and back of the hats, would not be so eager to caress now; but I will not insist a great deal upon a sort of sigh which has been often known in print already. I think it much more profitable to note that all the *entourage* of Niagara was then private property, and was put to those money-making uses at the expense of the public which form one of the holiest attributes of that sacred thing. I never greatly objected to the paper-mills on Goat Island; they were impertinent to the scenery, of course, but they were picturesque, with their low-lying, weather-worn masses in the shelter of the forest trees, beside the brawling waters. But nearly every other assertion of private rights in the landscape was an outrage to it. I will not even try to recall the stupid and squalid contrivances which defaced it at every point, and extorted a coin from the insulted traveler at every turn. They are all gone now, and in the keeping of the State the whole redeemed and disenthralled vicinity of Niagara is an object-lesson in what public ownership, whenever it comes, does for beauty.

I had the eagerness of a true believer to see this result, and even before I went to look at the cataract on my last visit a winter ago, I drove about and made sure from the liberated landscape that the people were in possession of their own. It was wonderful, even in mid-winter, the difference in dignity and prosperity that not so much appeared as seemed to reappear, and to find in the beholder's consciousness a sense of what that divine prospect must have been when the eye of the white man first gazed upon it. The landscape had got back something of its youth, and in my joy in it, I got back something of mine.

I do not say that I got much. At fifty, one is at least not twice as young as at twenty-five. But I was very fairly young again when I came to Niagara in the mid-winter of my mid-winter year, and I was certainly as impatient as I could have been quarter of a century earlier to see the ice-bridge below the Falls and the ice-cone that their breath had formed; in fact,

I had waited a good deal longer to see them. Shall I own that at first sight these were a disappointment? At first sight the Falls themselves are a disappointment, for we come to them with something other than the image of their grand and simple adequacy in our minds, and seek to match them with that distempered invention of the ignorant fancy. I had supposed the ice-cone was a sharp peak, jutting up in front of the cataract, not reflecting that it must be what it always is, a rounded knoll, built up finely, finely, slowly, slowly, out of the spectral shapes of mist, seized by the frost and flung down upon the frozen river. When you remember that this ice-cone is formed of the innumerable falls of these ghosts, I think one ought to be content with the Romanesque dome-shape of the mound, however Gothic one's expectation may have been. I do not deny that I should still prefer the pinnacle, but that is because I prefer Gothic architecture; and I advise the reader not to hope for it. If he has a pleasure in delicate decoration, the closely stippled slopes of the ice-cone will give it to him; it is like that fine jeweler's work on the grain of dead gold where the whole surface is fretted with infinitesimal points. When these catch the sun of such a blue mid-winter sky as lifted its speckless arch above the ice-cone on the day I saw it, the effect is all that one has a right to ask of mere nature. I am trying to hint that I would have built the ice-cone somewhat differently, if it had been left to me, but that I am not hypercritical. If it seems a little low, a little lumpish in the retrospect; still it had its great qualities, which I should be the last in refusing to recognize.

The name ice-bridge had deceived me, but the ice-bridge did not finally disappoint me. It is not a bridge at all. It is the channel of the river blocked as far as the eye can see down the gorge with huge squares and oblongs of ice, or of frozen snow, as they seem, and giving a realizing effect to all the remembered pictures of arctic scenery. This was curiously heightened by some people with sleds among the crowds, making their way through the ice pack from shore to shore; there wanted only the fierce dash of some Esquimaux dog-team and the impression would have been perfect. It was best to look down upon it all from the cliffs, when at times the effect was more than arctic, when it was lunar: you could fancy yourself gazing upon the face of a dead world, or rather a plaster mask of it, with these small black figures of people crawling over it like flies. It was perfectly still that day, and in spite of the diapason of the Falls, an inner silence possessed the air. From the cliffs along the river the cedars thrust outward, armored in plates of ice, like the immemorial effigies of old-time warriors, and every cascade that had flung its bannerol of mist to the summer air, was now furled to the face of the rock and frozen fast. Again a sense of the repose, which is the secret of Niagara's charm, filled me.

There was repose even in the peculiar traffic of

Niagara when we penetrated to a shop devoted to the sale of its bric-a-brac for some photographs of the winter scenery, and we fancied a weird surprise and a certain statuesque reluctance in the dealer. But this may have been merely our fancy. I would insist only upon the mute immobility of the birds on the feather fans behind the glazed shelves, and a mystical remoteness in the Japanese objects mingled with the fabrics of our own Indians and the imported feldspar cups and vases.

Our train went back to Buffalo through the early winter sunset, crimson and crimsoner over the rapids, and then purple over the ice where the river began to be frozen again. This color was so intense that the particles of ice along the brink were like a wilding growth of violets—those candied violets you see at the confectioner's.

WHAT TO SEE

A CONSECUTIVE DESCRIPTION FOR VISITORS

BY FREDERIC ALMY

1.

THE most greedy imagination need not remain long hungry at Niagara. A single well-used day, with a sun bright enough to start the rainbows, is enough to satisfy every expectation. And yet, many who see the Falls for the first time are disappointed, even in the case of people qualified to enjoy their beauty. No one can question Mrs. Jameson's keen appreciation of the beautiful, at least in art, but this is her statement of her first impressions: "I am no longer Anna,—I am metamorphosed,—I am translated,—I am an ass's head, a clod, a wooden spoon, a fat weed growing on Lethe's bank, a stock, a stone, a petrification,—for have I not seen Niagara, the wonder of wonders; and felt—no words can tell *what* disappointment!"

Many visitors have expressed the same feeling, as honestly if not so comically. There are various reasons for so general an experience, but no one of them implies any short-coming in the place itself. For instance, a rather stolid mind takes in such a sight slowly. One look is not enough to quicken it. A more sensitive temperament, on the other hand, is sure to come to Niagara with such composite anticipations that no single aspect of the place could satisfy them all.

The first view of Niagara comes only once. If you care to have it the best possible, it is worth while to choose your approach as carefully as a chess player chooses his opening. The best first view from the top of the bank is on the Canadian side; but if you have arrived by a railroad which leaves you on the American shore it is almost equally good to cross the Suspension Bridge and then walk up the other bank. You see the whole sweep of both Falls at once; at the left the American Fall with its width of 1060 feet, then Goat Island, with 1300 feet more, and on the right the Horse Shoe with a curve of 3010 feet; in all, a total width of a full mile. The fault of this view is that the great width dwarfs the height and makes the Falls seem very low indeed. The American Fall is 167 feet high, the Horse Shoe 158; and yet the effect is of a long, low wall.

The next best view from above, and the one generally seen first by visitors, is from the brink at Prospect Park, but here the Falls are seen in profile, and the line of their length is, as it were, foreshortened. Moreover, from either of these two chief points of first observation the height of the Falls seems much less than when they are seen from below. It is better to insist on seeing Niagara first from its base. What we look down on never seems so great as what we must look up to.

The weather and the season have their influence. A cloudy day will take away the rainbows, and on a chilly day you have to move along from spot to spot, and cannot loiter idly where you choose and live into the beauty of the place.

If you are easily moved it may be that a tremor of excitement will take possession of your senses as you approach Niagara for the first time, and so subdue your judgment that you will have no power to criticise; but, on the other hand, no matter how callous you may be, no matter how utter a Philistine, it is possible for you to be so introduced that you will be made an instantaneous convert to the majesty of the place if not to its beauty. If you are willing to take the climax of Niagara at the outset and so forestall every possibility of disappointment,—man or woman, if you have the heart of a man, and the courage to lay it, at once, bare, against the great heart of Niagara, I advise you without the least preliminary glance of any kind to enter the watery chaos of the Cave of the Winds.

WHAT TO SEE. 31

Cross the light bridge that leads to Goat Island, with the rapids of the American Fall slipping furiously under you as they fall from the sky line at the left; with the brink itself a few rods below you on the right, so that you see the plunge, but not the fall; with the roar of the torrent in your ears and the rank, musty smell of the roily water strong in your nostrils; and finally, before you in the distance, rising over the tree tops of Goat Island, the pillar of cloud by day that guards the Horse Shoe. If it is very early morning in midsummer, and the wind is favorable, a rainbow, zenith high, will overarch the scene, but this is hardly needed to quicken the pulses of your heart as you advance to meet the wonder of your thoughts from early childhood. Take now the middle path across the idyllic beauty of the island. You find it a cool bower, sweet with every wood fragrance, carpeted in the spring with masses of blue violets and white trillium, and overspread by branches of huge trees, whose leaves sift out the sunlight until it falls in patches only on the road below. It is a place in which to " loaf and invite the soul," as Whitman says, but now is not the time. Five minutes brings you to the dressing house that marks the entrance to the Cave of the Winds. Here it will take a strong will not to look down over the hand rail on the bank; but the epicure in sensations will refrain. Indeed, to look now is to spoil everything, and to accept for your first view of Niagara one of the least imposing of all. Instead, step quickly into the house, pay your dollar for the necessary escort of a guide, strip clean to the skin with no thought of retaining even your underclothes, and put on the homely and uncomfortable, but eminently practical suit that is offered you. A blouse and trousers of a light gray flannel, a hooded coat and overalls of yellow oilskin, and slippers made out of a sheet of thick white felt folded around the foot and firmly tied in place with strips of whip-cord—arrayed in these you are like a Gloucester sea-captain in a squall, or like an Esquimau in oilskin. Now throw around your neck a string to which is tied the key that locks the chest in which you have placed your valuables, let the boy in attendance tie about your waist more whip-cord for a sash, and then, in full court costume, you are ready to be presented to Majesty.

To reach the cave you circle down the cliff by an uncomfortable, small, winding staircase, of a sort familiar to sight-seers abroad. From this you presently emerge, out of breath, upon a ledge of rock, with the dark green waters of the river just below and a vertical wall of granite towering far above. Now, from above, the only way thoroughly to enjoy a precipice is to lie flat upon your face and peer over the edge downward. This is impracticable at Niagara; but from below the height is appreciated keenly as the eye toils upward along the face of the cliff in its effort to find a horizon. Figures seen at the sky-line appear one-half their actual size.

A mere score of steps now brings you around a curve and puts before your sight the enormous sheet of water, vast in itself, but at Niagara insignificant and inconspicuous, which curtains the Cave of the Winds. About one hundred and fifty feet in height, and as much in breadth, it descends between Goat Island and Luna Island. It has no special name, and the ordinary visitor to Niagara will hardy realize its separate existence. Our English cousins who do not go behind it may respect it more if they are told that it leaves the sky at the height of the top of the western towers of Canterbury or of Durham Cathedrals, and that it has twice the width of the main facade of either. If they have ever been behind they need no details to ensure respect. We see it first in profile, a long, curving edge of green and white, not so much falling from the brink above as leaping, with a forward plunge, so that between its inner wall and the retreating surface of the cliff is left a strange gray cavern, now to be explored.

I have been through the cave a score of times, but no number of trips can ever dull or in any degree displace in my mind the impressions of the first visit. In quiet ignorance of what was to come I approached the precipitous wooden stair-case which descends behind the fall. Looking across I saw a patch of blue sky at the farther outlet of the cave, but elsewhere all the air was dark with criss-crossed blasts of sleet, hurtling in all directions like frightened comets. A second later the battery of the fall was on my head and all the Powers of the Air were at my throat. Around my feet a rainbow formed a ring through which I seemed to drop into blackness. The staircase stopped and I was on a narrow ledge of rock, with no more path or rail, hugging myself against a slippery wall of stone. The water clutched my feet furiously. Neither the burly guide nor the stranger who had accompanied me was to be seen. I started to go forward, but as I turned a mass of water struck me breathless. I tried to find the stairs, but a worse dash of water from the other side outdid the first. Facing the wall again I waited, perhaps thirty seconds, wondering, when suddenly the guide appeared with the frightened Frenchman whom he had pursued to the top of the stairs, and there recaptured. It was a lonesome introduction to the place, but we moved on now together through the water, clinging desperately with our toes through the felt to whatever foothold we could discover, and glad to have the support of our hands as well as feet. Dignity in such a place, and such a costume, is the last thing to be considered. Half blinded, quite deafened, gasping,—the agitation of the nerves is too great at first for observation; but

A bit of the American Falls from below the Cave of the Winds—Winter.

soon the eye learns how to follow the curving inner surface of the falling water, half translucent and of shifting colors, far up to where it leaves the line of the cliff above. It learns to overcome the twilight and gather outlines of black, terraced rocks, dripping with streams of sleet, that form the amphitheatre of the cave. You learn to step fearlessly into the churning water, towards the Fall, knowing that the rebound of the cataract is so violent that even if you lost your footing you would only be thrust roughly back against the terraces. It is soon over. A brief climb up the ledges brings you to dry rock and the bright sun again, but you have seen a cave of Æolus such as Virgil never dreamed of. Henceforth the lines in the opening pages of the Æneid :

*Hic vasto rex Æolus antro
Luctantes ventos vinclis et carcere frenat,*
will have new meaning.

A clever writer lately said* that the cave was like a small choky corridor with the deluge going on inside it, and he marvelled greatly that the end of his trip coincided with the point of departure and did not occur *in transitu.* In fact, like my French comrade, he arrived simultaneously at the entrance to the cave and the conclusion that he had had enough. Many men do the same, but hardly ever a woman, though women frequently go through the cave. It is alarm-

---
* John J. à Becket, in Harper's Weekly for May 30, 1891.

ing but not dangerous, and accidents are almost unheard of.

There is no surer way to take the conceit out of a complacent cockney who affects to look down on Niagara than to make him run this gauntlet. I think always of Emerson's lines on Monadnoc :

> Pants up hither the spruce clerk
> From South Cove and City Wharf.
> I take him up my rugged sides,
> Half-repentant, scant of breath,—
> *   *   *   *   *   *
> I scowl on him with my cloud,
> With my north wind chill his blood ;
> I lame him, clattering down the rocks ;
> And to live he is in fear.
> Then, at last, I let him down
> Once more into his dapper town,
> To chatter, frightened, to his clan
> And forget me if he can.

The passage through the cave is an experience too grim and colorless for pure pleasure, but the return across the rocks in front of the fall—in a bright sun— is a luxury of delight. The heart that "leaps up when it beholds a rainbow in the sky" will here be in a dancing fever of excitement, for there are whole rainbows, half rainbows and quarter rainbows, not in the sky, distant and inaccessible, but in your fingers, around your head and between your feet, while the pot of gold at the rainbow's foot is a caldron of molten silver, foaming and rushing about your knees, and tugging at you with an invitation that is irresistible. I have seen grave men frolic in the water, their trousers and sleeves swelled almost to bursting with the imprisoned air; now clenching their toes firmly in some crevice and leaning back with all their force against the cushion of water that rocked them like a cradle; now crouching low with arms akimbo while the interrupted stream sprang high above their heads in an arching curve, like a sea shell around a naiad; now thrusting themselves into invisibility against some rock over which the torrent broke in a noisy cascade,—their heads safe in the airhole near the crest, from which they dimly watched the passing figures in their oil skins, until they chose to startle them by re-appearing. To play so with Niagara brings an exhilaration that is indescribable. It "washes brain and heart clean" and gives a child's courage for the tasks of the world. The exaltation is heightened by the heavy roar of the cataract close above you, and the brilliant beauty of color all around you. You climb through one circular rainbow to the top of a black boulder and descend through another on the other side; you cross slippery wooden bridges, exposed to such furious castigation from the sleet that you bend involuntarily in homage to the fearful power of your recent playfellow. Most glorious of all, whenever for a moment the eye is not so buffeted by driving spray as to deprive you entirely of your vision, look upwards, always upwards—where the flashing peaks of the American Fall tower above the deluge like the snowy summits of a mountain chain.

> In such access of mind, in such high hour
> Of visitation from the living God,
> Thought is not, in enjoyment it expires,—
> Rapt into still communion that transcends
> The imperfect offices of prayer and praise.

II.

The Maid of the Mist.—The Horse Shoe.

Everywhere at Niagara the genius of the place has many different moods. Often at the Cave of the Winds there is not a rainbow; sometimes when the spray beats down the river you can even enter the cave without a wetting. It may take twenty different trips to see all its splendor, but fully to see it once is worth them all. I know of nothing in Nature to be compared with it. The valley of the Rhone Glacier at dusk, when the white frozen mass of ice falls silently at your feet from the sky above, suggests it dimly, but only as the moon in daylight suggests the sun. For many, though, the pleasures of the cave are too robust. All such should still attempt to see Niagara first from below, and the next best way is from the steamer called the Maid of the Mist.

The approach is through Prospect Park, and by taking the central path to the inclined railway you can again reach the water's edge without so much as one glimpse of the Fall. As you come out of the house at the foot of the railway there is a territory at your left, full of attractions, but your way lies to the right. From the steamer landing you see a broad river of a dark green color, its surface glassy as a mirror, as placid and unruffled as if it had never known a struggle or a fall. Men swim in it with safety. Before you is the disappointing profile of the upper half of the American Fall. The lower half is hid by rocks and spray. Slip on one of the rubber cloaks in the saloon, take a rubber blanket, and rush forward to the choice seats at the very front of the upper deck. As the steamer moves sturdily forward, still through smooth green water, the air begins to fill with a soft spray, as fine and penetrating as a Scotch mist, and the water is thickly overlaid with foam. You coast along the one thousand and sixty feet of the American Fall, close to the rocks below and so very close to the Fall itself that it is almost terrifying. Nothing is distinctly seen, for the eyes blink in the beating rain. You can see better if you wear glasses; the wet glass dims them, but you can at least keep your eyes open more steadily. Nothing is distinctly heard. The deep note of Niagara sounds in your ears with a heavy throb that is almost painful. You are confronted by a rippling, flashing, shimmering wall of white, a precipice of falling foam, furrowed in deep creases by the uneven contour of the brink, and rebounding high in a leaping cloud of spray that always hides the base from every eye. Near the steamer are many boulders; the largest the Rock of Ages that stands before the entrance to the Cave of the Winds. Then come the bare cliffs of Goat Island, another thousand feet or more; and then,—the Horse Shoe. Its lofty curving walls confront each other, one hundred and sixty feet in height, and in their contour fully three thousand feet, or more than half a mile. The plucky Maid pushes straight into this pit of falling waters; forward she goes, into its depths, until for an instant, for one short second, there is nothing to the right, to the left, or before, nothing anywhere in the whole world for you but the enclosing cataracts falling on all sides from the sky. It is just one second of crowded, glorious life, worth a year's pilgrimage. The little steamer has gone as far as the full force of her engines will carry her; she lurches heavily, tosses like a cork on the white surging foam, wheels suddenly around, and shoots like an arrow down the stream and away.

The views now are from the stern; first of the rapidly receding Horse Shoe, then of Goat Island, then of the American Fall as we coast again along its length, nearly as closely as before, and finally, from the Canadian dock, a panorama of both Falls. From here the boat returns to the American landing, but the tourist's best plan is to go ashore, climb the Canadian bank by the winding road, and either walk or ride along the crest of the cliff to Inspiration Point and to the former site of Table Rock.

It is disappointing to the patriotic soul, but not to be disputed, that the finest views of Niagara are to be had on the Canadian side. Goat Island, the Three Sisters, Prospect Park, the Rapids and the River Road are all exceedingly beautiful. Perhaps there is more variety of beauty in the American Park than in the other, but when you have seen it all there is no place to which you come back so eagerly for rest and inspiration as to Table Rock and the Canadian shore. It is not the best first view, as has been said, for the rampart of Niagara is a mile in width, and, seen from a distance and from above, looks like a long, low wall. But for a final view, or a view to rest with, it has no equal.

The Queen Victoria Park was not established until 1888, or three years after the State of New York had purchased Goat Island and the land on the American side, and dedicated it to its people. Here and there are trifling indications of the different temper of the governments on either bank. Take for instance the governmental sign boards with their warning notices, which in Canada are less considerate of the tender feelings of the dear public than with us. Mark the autocratic barbarity of the British declaration that persons throwing stones over the bank will be prosecuted according to law, as compared with the exquisite delicacy of the placards that meet you at every turn on Goat Island: "Do Not Venture in Dangerous Places." "Do Not Harm the Trees and Shrubs." "*Stones Thrown Over the Bank May Fall upon People Below.*" On Goat Island you feel always as if your mother were with you.

The Queen Victoria Park is much more trig than its neighbor. It has flower beds and close clipped lawns, rustic arbors and wigwams, busts of notables, and even fountains! In the State Reservation, on the contrary, the more important portions are in a condition almost primeval. Goat Island is still covered with original forest, except for the carriage ways and foot-paths that traverse its area. That this is so is due no doubt to the fortunate fact that for generations all the Niagara islands as well as part of the mainland were owned by the wealthy family of Gen. Peter B. Porter, well known in the War of 1812. A summer hotel on the bank of Goat Island, overlooking the Horse Shoe, would have been a source of enormous profit, but the sanctity of the place was never invaded. A pleasant story is told of one of the family who was asked in England if she had ever seen Niagara Falls. Drawing herself up proudly, she quite annihilated her questioner with the unexpected answer: "Niagara Falls! I *own* them."

It is well to remind the visitor that in distributing his time the hours given to the Canadian Park should be in the afternoon. At Niagara, Canada is the land of the setting sun, and it is only in the afternooon that the superb bows can be seen which rise high in the sky, sometimes over-arching both Falls in a single curve. It is the other shore which is distinctly Rainbow Land. Give only the sun, and on the American shore the wise pilgrim can have his rainbow, be it morning or be it afternoon. In the morning at Prospect Park if the day is clear one rainbow is certain, two are usual, and to see three concentric bows, each reversing the colors of its neighbor, is not uncommon. At the brink of the Horse Shoe it is the same, while in the afternoon I know of no more beautiful sight at Niagara than the view of Luna Island and the great American Fall, framed by an iridescent bow.

Suppose, then, that it is the afternoon. You make your way along the Canadian shore towards Inspiration Point, and what we still call Table Rock, though the last vestige of the rock itself fell over forty years ago. You find at once that here the railroad has entered Paradise. The tracks of an electric road accompany you all the way. It was built in 1892, and runs along the whole Niagara gorge from Queenston, seven miles below, to the placid beauty of the Dufferin Islands, where iron railroad bridges now run side by side with all the older ones of inoffensive wood. The world must move. Electric cars run from The Hague to the bathing houses of Scheveningen. They run even from Florence to Fiesole, and how can Niagara be spared. They are necessary and laudable, but to the eye as unattractive as the cheap books that have opened literature to the million.

Below Inspiration Point the view may possibly be disappointing, but from this point on it is difficult for one who knows the place to see how even a newcomer can fail to be most powerfully impressed, especially if the conviction of the height of Niagara has been first well driven home by a journey through the Cave or on the steamer. Still, a Bostonian looked first from here and promptly wished to improve on Nature by removing the barren wall of Goat Island, so that there should be one continuous fall. A more legitimate and not infrequent source of disappointment is due to the heavy spray. Over and over travellers brought with care to Table Rock for their first view, open their eyes to see only an invisible Niagara, both American Fall and the Horse Shoe being veiled completely by a loud thundering cloud of mist.

Ordinarily, however, as you advance towards the Horse Shoe, and see farther and farther into its white recesses until at Table Rock you are admitted almost to the heart of its secrets, the sensation of awe in the presence of such majesty is irresistible. You stand at one limit of the vast curve. Your eye traverses the whole extent of the silent sheets of plunging water, and follows them downward to the milky sea beneath. From below rise such enormous clouds of shifting spray that at times all outlines are confused. The vagueness magnifies each distance, and through the blur the opposite crest seems infinitely far away, and the chasm bottomless. The effect is all of white and gray, and yet conspicuous before you is the great Green Water, the one place where the flood of Niagara does not break instantly into foam but clings together in a solid sheet that descends for many feet unbroken, exhibiting the exquisite color of the green deep sea. The water nearer is sometimes turbid and yellow. Everywhere its surface has a waxen, sheeny glaze that is characteristic of Niagara. At the convergence of the two opposite faces of the cataract the confusion of waters is indescribable. Above all mounts the white column of spray that seems to

" Rise like a cloud of incense from the earth."

The man or woman here who does not descend to the foot of the precipice commits a sin unpardonable. Fear may forbid the Cave of the Winds, or even the Maid of the Mist, but here you have firm Mother-earth to stand on. If the whim of the wind allows you dry rocks you can lie at your ease in the sun and drink in almost the view which the prow of the steamer presents for a second and then snatches from you. You are in the same white pit of downward rushing walls. You have almost the same sense of having conquered the inaccessible, of having invaded sanctity. It is like the disembodied joys of spirits.

Mr. Howells has spoken of the *repose* of Niagara. Another paradox is its silence. The sheets of falling water are so unchanging to the eye that the motion seems no more actual than when the breeze runs through a field of grain. It moves without moving. In some such way the unchanging volume of sound soon leaves on the ear a strange sense of silence. Now and again, however, as some more compact mass of water makes its fall, a new note strikes the ear, and under all is the heavy beating of the air as if of sound too low for the range of human hearing. It has always seemed to me as if much of the voice of Niagara might be to us inaudible.*

It is strange that no great poem has yet been written for Niagara. Many have tried their hand, but there is nothing of established fame, nothing that is known for itself as well as for its subject. There is line after line, however, of Coleridge's Hymn to Mont Blanc which if once thought of at Niagara will be always thought of there. Verse after verse is curiously apposite. Those who have never made the translation from mountain to cataract will find in it a wealth of new associations for both poem and place.

---

* In Scribner's Magazine for February, 1881, there is an article on "The Music of Niagara," by Eugene M. Thayer. He writes the chords of its different harmonics, but finds them *four octaves* lower than the key boards of our pianos.

The waters at thy base
Rave ceaselessly ; but thou, most awful Form,
[Fallest] from forth thy silent sea of green,
How silently. . . . .
O dread and silent [Fall !] I gazed upon thee
Till thou, still present to the bodily sense,
Didst vanish from my thought. Entranced in prayer
I worshipped the Invisible alone.

Yet like some sweet beguiling melody,
So sweet we know not we are listening to it,
Thou, the meanwhile, wast blending with my thought,—
Yea, with my life and life's own secret joy—
Till the dilating soul, enrapt, transfused,
Into the mighty vision passing—there,
As in her natural form, swelled vast to Heaven.
*   *   *   *   *   *   *   *   *
Who gave you your invulnerable life,
Your strength, your speed, your fury, and your joy,
Unceasing thunder and eternal foam ?
*   *   *   *   *   *   *   *   *
Who made you glorious as the gates of Heaven
Beneath the keen full moon ? Who bade the sun
Clothe you with rainbows ? Who, with living flowers
Of loveliest blue, spread garlands at your feet ?
God !—let the torrents, like a shout of nations,
Answer ! and let the ice-plains echo, God !

III.

The Islands—The Rapids—The American Shore.

The Titans of Niagara have been presented. They are grand, beautiful, but overpowering. The strain on the sensations is so exhausting that to stay long with them is oppressive. You look your fill and then are more than glad to withdraw to the more human pleasures of the islands. Above the Horse Shoe on the Canadian shore the Dufferin Islands are the perfection of rustic loveliness. They are just a tangled cluster of wooded islands, with thin gray sheets of swift water rushing around them, but they are exquisite. There are Lovers' Walks, and bowers, and platforms, and on the outskirts the open, breezy river, and the sweep of the White Horse rapids. The American islands, however, are anchored in the very centre of Niagara. Two of them, Luna Island and Goat Island, are on the brink of the Fall, and the latter of these is a famous treasure-house of delights. You circle round it by a shady road with cool forest depths on one side and on the other a steep, wooded bank with glimpses of the river through the leaves. A flight of steps leads down to Luna Island, and from its landings affords the finest view that is to be had of the American Fall. If you study it closely you will find that there are subtle harmonies in the color of Niagara as well as in its music. The Fall is by no means only gray and white. If the sun favors, you will find at times faint tints of lavender, of rose, and green.

A low bridge leads directly over the roof of the Cave of the Winds to Luna Island. This bridge in winter is so thickly crusted with ice that as you cross your feet are almost level with the railing at the side. The island itself is so called from the lunar rainbow which is often seen from it in the spray,—a mere, dim ghost of a rainbow, hardly brighter than the third arch even of a solar bow. It is beautiful to see, but the beauty lies less in the bow itself than in its weird accompaniment of night shadows and moonlight. The island is small, and so flat upon the water that a trifle would submerge it. The shallow transparent sheet of water that passes over the long ragged edge of the American Fall is so near your feet that you can touch it as it leaves the brink.

In fact, everywhere the great accessibility of Niagara is strongly felt. It never holds you at arms length. From the opposite bank, at Prospect Park, it is the same. As you look down at the huge clouds of smoky vapor you lean over a low parapet of stone along which the river brushes as it makes the plunge; and if you continue now along the Goat Island road to the Horse Shoe you can paddle in the water at the very verge. There is never the tantalizing wish to get " a little nearer." Except for occasional dashes of spray, no monarch of Nature allows more absolute freedom of approach.

From Goat Island, the Horse Shoe shows but one of its curving faces, but it is that which is crowned by the wonderful Green Water already mentioned. It is better seen from the bank above than from below.

The rich green mass descends unbroken until it is lost to sight behind the nearer curve of the Fall. You see no chasm; merely two edges with a deep seam or scar between, broken at moments by a sudden, spurting leap of spray from the invisible depths, a silent messenger of the tumult below.

The road leaves the Horse Shoe. A broad, breezy view fills the eye, and presently appear the iron bridges of the Three Sister Islands. The first bridge crosses a thin stream of water, so quiet that no one would be afraid to wade to the other side. There is no suggestion of the rush and roar of Niagara. The second stream is much more turbulent. The third, narrow but noisy, comes racing down the slope with breathless speed, and crashes immediately over a low parapet of rock with an uproar as of forty Niagaras. It is so little and so furious that it frightens you. It shakes the water into shreds and tatters and flings it down in a tangled heap of white motion, to pass on instantly without reprieve to the new fate beyond. It is like torture before death. A soft green dimple in the lower stream is all that marks the vortex of the Horse Shoe into which the water plunges

The small bridge quivers with the rush of water so close below it. This bridge and Prospect Park are said to be the favorite resorts of men intent on suicide, but those who care for life can hardly find a dearer lingering spot for a long summer's day than at the foot of this small torrent.

The Third Sister gives again the broad, free outlook on the river. Not far from the shore is the Spouting Rock, or Leaping Horse, where the water shoots up at intervals in a dash of spray. A little clambering over the rocks of the island brings you to the water's edge, where you can look up the current to the horizon. By springing over a narrow gap you reach a boulder near the shore, on the farther side of which the water sweeps down a little glassy shoot shaped like a beaver's tail. Tiny white waves keep curling up it from below, trying to climb the slope. The pigmy army is unwearied in its attack, but, like Sisyphus, it toils upward in vain.

The carriage road and foot path lead from the Sisters to the Parting of the Waters at the upper end of Goat Island, where the river divides its mass for either Fall very quietly, with only a light ripple on the shore; and still farther is a glen known as "The Spring." Then come the bridges to the main land, and the tour of Goat Island has been accomplished.

It is late to speak of the famous rapids above Goat Island bridge. To half the visitors of Niagara they are the chief source of pleasure. To see them it is necessary, absolutely, to descend to one of the platforms at the river's edge. Unless you do so they have not been seen. Sit half an hour, at least, watching, and the fascination will seize you irresistibly. It is like a great turmoil of tossing ostrich feathers, except that there is feverish life in these white plumes, restlessly curling. There are tags of verse in the mind everywhere at Niagara. The one that speaks to me here is from Matthew Arnold:

> Now the wild white horses play,
> Champ and chafe and toss in the spray.

And again:

> The wild white horses foam and fret,
> "Margaret! Margaret!"

In sunshine these rapids blaze from a distance like white fire and are intolerable to the eye. Beyond them, at the water's edge, is a willow grove which gives again the constant alternation between peace and conflict that makes Niagara so bewildering; and if you wish in full measure a benediction on your day, return to the train by the lovely River Road which follows the bank in an easy curve that is a delight to the senses. It is but a moment longer to the station, and I know of nothing that will leave so sweet a flavor in the mind.

IV.

Lower Niagara—The Whirlpool Rapids and Whirlpool—Lewiston.

All this—Cave of the Winds, Maid of the Mist and all—may be seen in a day by the abject slave to time. He will come away dazed, uncertain, almost, whether the cataract flows up or down, and unfit, utterly, to say a word in criticism, either of praise or blame. Still, if a day is all that life allows you, it is best to crowd it full.

Even the one-day tourist, if not afraid of mental indigestion, can make room in his day for all this, and yet find time for a glimpse, too, of lower Niagara.

Ten minutes by trolley, five by the train, take you to the village of Suspension Bridge, the Whirlpool Rapids, and the Whirlpool. Rather than these, however, if you are pressed for time, take the open observation cars of the New York Central through the gorge, to Lewiston. You will not be able to cross off the Whirlpool from your list of sights accomplished, but the deep gorge of the Niagara to Lake Ontario is more worth seeing. If time allows, however, see them all, especially the lower rapids.

The Whirlpool Rapids are wilder, finer, in every way more splendid than the rapids above the Falls. You go down Buttery's elevator (the other is less good), and at the foot between high walls of rock you find a mass of roaring water that leaps incredibly into the air. Seen from the bank it sometimes hides a low house on the other shore. The place is one to linger at for hours, and is one of the chief glories of the Falls. In trying to swim these rapids Captain Webb was drowned. Here all the army of cranks pass through in barrels. Here, too, in 1886, a modest Boston policeman, William J. Kendall, swam through with only a life preserver to protect him.

From the rapids if you are adventurous you can reach the Whirlpool by following the shore and climbing up the bank. If more prudent or in haste, you take the elevator as before, and then the road. Through the inevitable bazaar of curiosities you pass to the grounds of the Whirlpool. As you look down over the bank the first sensation is surprising, almost uncanny. Niagara is caught in a trap. It enters a circle without outlet. Your eye follows the whole contour and finds no interruption in the line of shore. From a few steps farther to the right you see below you the narrow gap through which the river turns, at a full right angle with its former course. It seems as if a girl could throw a stone across, but men have tried and seen the stone land on the nearer shore, short of the water's edge.

Those who expect to find a maelstrom in the Pool will be ludicrously taken by surprise. No country mill pond could be more serene. The water circles lazily around its pen as if indifferent whether it escaped or not. Above the hole and below is the rattle of the rapids and the glitter of their white spray, but the Whirlpool itself is dark and still. When the first disappointment is over at not seeing the boiling, riotous whirl of the railway posters, you realize a silent strength and majesty that grow awful. It is not so hard to believe that what is once drawn down into its center will not emerge for days.

To catalogue the pleasures of Niagara and not describe the many tramps it offers would be a great mistake. The shortest and perhaps the best is down the gorge to Lewiston, about five miles, a very easy journey for an afternoon. Begin not at Niagara but at Suspension Bridge. Two miles of country road lead to the Devil's Hole, the scene in 1765 of a massacre of English by the French and Indians who forced them down the cliff. Upon a broad plateau of rocks you look down on the tops of trees that fill the pit below. The rapids of the river spot its dark green surface with white, and their clamor is always in the air. A few steps farther on you leave the road, from which there are no views, and take the railroad track, a ledge half way up the side of the cliff, with a sheer mountain of rocks above and the wonderful river talking loudly below. Keep on the track to Lewiston and then come back by train; or if you have a whole day's time and can stand a more vigorous walk, begin on the Canadian side of the Suspension Bridge, walk by the road to the Whirlpool, crawl around its circling beach over ground thick with petrified leaves, and when you reach the outlet climb somehow up the bluff and keep to the brink until you reach Brock's Monument and Queenston. It is perhaps seven miles, and if you are rowed across at the Queenston ferry and come back up the railroad track from Lewiston you will have had a glorious day. The walk along the Canadian brink is tangled and rough, and often lengthened by retreating gorges which have to be skirted, but the views are beautiful. There are many jutting bluffs, and in the gorges are fantastic boulders. Upon the hill below the monument to General Brock you look far off to Lake Ontario; it is another place for a day's resting.

If you take this for an epilogue to Niagara you may like also a prologue. There is no pleasanter approach than to walk or drive from Buffalo on the Canadian shore. The distance is not more than twenty miles and the road is almost always at the water's edge almost upon the beach.

V.

Seasons and Moods.

The perfect time for the trip to Lewiston is in October. The Canadian bank is then a blaze of flame, and the green river below and blue sky above make a beautiful color picture. The most lovely time for upper Niagara is in early spring, when Goat Island is covered with flowers and the trees show every tender shade of green. The most wonderful season is, however, undoubtedly mid-winter.

Niagara in winter is like a fairy tale come true. The spray gathers and freezes so incessantly that twigs the size of knitting needles are cased with ice until they have the bigness of a squirrel's tail. Whole bushes are so covered, with a heavy splendor that pins them to the earth. A low sun flashing through this ice turns it to jewels. It is as if the rainbows of Niagara were flung before you in a tangled heap.

Below the American Fall the ice cone gathers and grows to the height of seventy-five or even of a hundred feet. Men climb it with spiked shoes and coast fearlessly down. The freezing spray covers your hat with enamel and makes your overcoat a rigid board.

Once in three or four years a so-called ice bridge forms. A warm day melts the field of ice above the Falls. It crashes down and chokes together in the narrow gorge below, forming an ice floe like a bridge from shore to shore. This bridge becomes a second Ponte Vecchio. It is lined at once on either side by mushroom booths where peddlers sell their wares. They take your tintype with Niagara for a background, but those who lend themselves to such an insult to the place are usually satisfied to sit before a hideous pasteboard scene although Niagara itself is close at hand. The merchants deal in foreign liquor upon the doubtful international line.

The ice bridge in itself is only this. It is its association with the winter scenery, and the vantage ground it gives for novel points of view, that make it well worth seeing. In winter usually you miss the charm of lazy summer lingering, but on the ice bridge you change the fleeting views the Maid of the Mist affords for ones more at your ease. You walk sturdily where you will, and look till you are satisfied. The pleasure, too, is greater at the water's edge than on a steamer's deck. Just so in summer it is pleasantest to cross by a small row-boat that ferries passengers.

It is not only the seasons that change the aspect of Niagara. In fact it differs every day in mood. You cannot go twice to the same place without seeing some new thing. One day you can climb higher than ever before upon the rocks at the base of Prospect Park until you sit dry in the shadow of the American Fall, fairly behind its sheet. Another day you cannot put your head outside of the house at the foot of the inclined railway without meeting a blinding shower of spray from the same Fall that makes any visit to the rocks impossible. These changes of the spray occur with disconcerting suddenness, especially below. The wind whips suddenly around the compass and before you think lashes the spray at your face. I have seen a girl who stood too near the Fall drenched instantly with such a rush of spray that everything upon her was wet through. Even when above a little wetting often comes.

These are the natural aspects of Niagara. To see it in more unfamiliar, curious beauty, as only one in hundreds cares to do, walk by summer moonlight through the Lewiston gorge or see the Horse Shoe by the winter moon.

To read too much of a place before seeing it is to prepare the way for disappointment. Unconsciously you expect to crowd into the first impression all the finest aspects of repeated visits made by others in their happiest moods. You are in danger, too, of displacing your own natural sensations by others ready made. A descriptive guide book stunts perception as often as it stimulates it. The purpose of this sketch lies in the hope that, just as a word may kindle memories and enrich itself in the mind of the hearer, these details may serve for a nucleus around which the scattering recollections of the place may gather more distinctly.

One final word. If after all, with all the time you have, Niagara disappoints you, pray have the grace to remember that the fault may be your own. In a sense you can see in it only what you bring with you. As has been said, if no man is a hero to his valet it is not perhaps because the hero is no hero, but because the valet is only a valet.

STATISTICS.

Niagara. Said to be an Iroquois word, meaning "Thunderer of Waters."

Niagara River.

Width, above the Falls, about 4,400 feet; below the Falls, about 1,000 feet; at the Whirlpool, about 400 feet.

Length of river, from Lake Erie to Lake Ontario, 36 miles.

Descent, from lake to lake, 336 feet, as follows: from Lake Erie to the Falls, (22 miles,) 70 feet, (55 feet of this in the Rapids, ½ mile); at the Falls, 160 feet; from the Falls to Lake Ontario, (14 miles), 106 feet.

Current, estimated at from 4 miles per hour in the quietest places to 40 miles at the Whirlpool Rapids.

Depth, estimated at 20 feet in the river above the Falls; at the Whirlpool Rapids, 250 feet; in the Whirlpool, 400 feet.

Volume. Estimated that 15,000,000 cubic feet of water per minute pass over the Falls, or about one cubic mile per week.

Niagara Falls.

Width of Falls at the brink, including Goat Island, 5,370 feet, as follows: American Falls, 1,060 feet; Goat Island, about 1,300 feet; the Horse Shoe, in 1890, 3,010 feet.

The Horse Shoe Falls.

Height, 158 feet. Contour, in 1890, 3,010 feet; in 1886, 2,600 feet; in 1842, 2,260 feet. Width across, at widest point, about 1,200 feet. Depth of water at brink, estimated 20 feet.

Average annual recession, 2.18 feet; total recession from 1842 to 1890, 104½ feet. Total area of recession for the same 48 years, 6⅓ acres.

The American Fall.

Height, 167 feet. Contour, in 1890, 1,060 feet; in 1842, 1,080 feet. Average annual recession, 7½ inches; total recession from 1842 to 1890, 30¾ feet. Total area of recession for same period, ¾ acre.

The New York State Reservation.

Area, 107 acres. Purchased by the State of New York, under Acts of April 30, 1883, and April 30, 1885, for $1,433,429.50: formally opened to the public July 15, 1885.

The Queen Victoria Niagara Falls Park.

Area, 154 acres. Preliminary Act of Legislature passed 1885. Park opened to the public, May 24, 1888.

Goat Island.

Area, about 63 acres; in early records said to have contained 250 acres. (Gull Island, south of Goat Island, is said to have contained two acres of land in 1840. There is hardly a trace of it now.) Circumference of island, about one mile. First bridge built, 1817; present bridge, 1856.

Bridges to Three Sister Islands built 1868.

The price paid by the State of New York for Goat Island and all the surrounding Islands except a part of Bath Island, was $525,000.00.

Suspension Bridge.

Height of floor above river, 190 feet; height of

towers, 100 feet; length of span, 1268 feet. First built, 1868-69; blown down and rebuilt, 1889.

Steamers " Maid of the Mist."

First boat built and run, 1846. Larger boat built, 1854. Ran the Whirlpool and Rapids to Lewiston, to escape the sheriff, 1861. First of present boats launched, 1885, 71 feet long; second launched, 1892, 85 feet long.

CHARGES.

Within New York State Reservation.

Inclined Railway, Prospect Park. Either way, 5 cents. Stairs free.

Steamers " Maid of the Mist," with rubber coat, 50 cents.

Cave of the Winds, guide and dress, $1.00.

Within Canadian Reservation.

Behind Horse Shoe Falls, with guide and dress, 50 cents.

Dufferin Islands, 50 cents for carriage and all occupants, 10 cents for pedestrian.

Suspension Bridge.

Upper bridge, over and back, 25 cents. Lower bridge, two miles below, over and back, 10 cents.

Whirlpool.

American or Canadian side, 50 cents.

Whirlpool Rapids.

American or Canadian side, with elevator, 50 cents.

Brock's Monument, 185 feet high; built 1853. A

WHAT TO SEE. 63

former monument, 126 feet high, built in 1826, was destroyed by explosion in 1840. Gen. Brock fell in 1813. Admission to top of monument, 50 cents.

CARRIAGE HIRE.

N. Y. Reservation Omnibuses.

Round trip, including circuit of Goat Island, with stop-overs, 25 cents. Shorter trips with stop-overs, 15 cents. Children under twelve years, half fare. Children under five years, free.

Carriage Rates by Niagara Falls Ordinances.

Two horses, first hour $2.00, each additional hour $1.50. One horse, first hour $1.50, each additional hour $1.00.

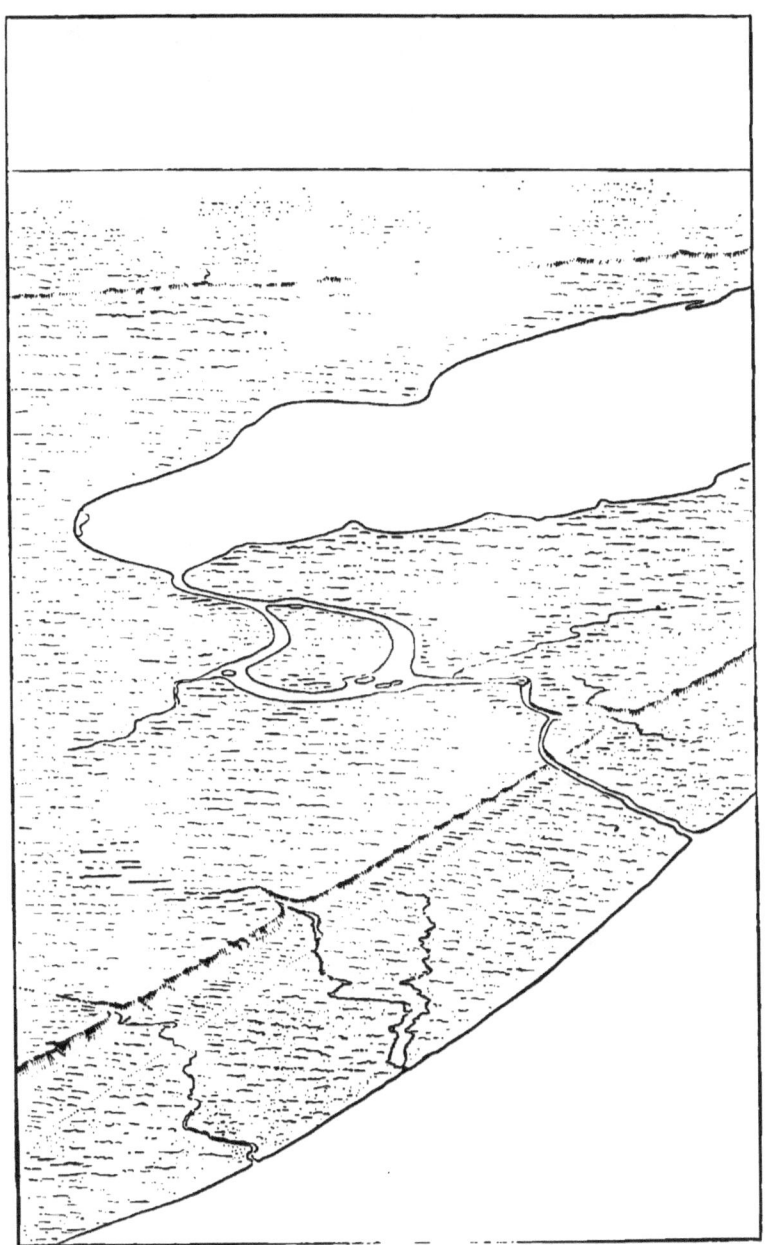

Bird's-eye view of Niagara River.

The Geology of Niagara Falls
BY
Prof. N. S. Shaler.
Dean of the Lawrence Scientific School, Harvard University.

THE effect of the more majestic spectacles of nature is to turn the mind of the observer away from the philosophy of the events which he is observing. This is a natural and wholesome action of all splendid things; he is indeed happy who flies at once to speculation as to the cause of that which he for the first time freely beholds. There is, however, a second stage in the service which the great spectacles of the earth can do for us. This is where we seek to understand the ways in which the offering is made to our souls. The well-trained naturalist, indeed any one who is attentive to the æsthetic as well as the rational opportunities of the world, learns in a manner to combine these impressions which may come to him by instinctive appreciation and by knowledge. To him the beautiful and the magnificent are none the less moving because he sees them in the perspective of history, or in the great assemblage of causations. It is the fairest province of science to afford these accessories of understanding so that the beauty of nature may make a deeper impression upon the mind of man.

Its work should in no wise diminish our perception or esteem of the beautiful; it should in fact unite these motives with our ordinary thought. Therefore it seems fit that we should consider the lessons which may be derived from a study of this great water-fall.

The first step towards the comprehension of any such feature as Niagara Falls should lead the student to an understanding of a general kind as to the range of the phenomena with which it is allied. We will therefore begin our inquiry by a brief consideration as to the various kinds of water-falls, and the conditions which produce them. It is easy to recognize the truth that all streams tend to form continuous and uninterrupted slopes down which their waters course from the highlands to the sea. It is to this principle, indeed, that we owe the fact that nearly all great rivers are freely navigable, and the most of the lesser are, for the greater part of their length, fit for small boats. Wherever we find a river in the tumult of a water-fall or of a cascade we readily note that it is steadfastly engaged in destroying the obstruction, and that given geologic time enough it will wear a channel down which its waters may glide quietly to the deep whence they came, and to which they inevitably return. If a new continent should be elevated, and rivers formed upon it, they would quickly develop a host of waterfalls. If the continent were high, it would be a land of cascades. Gradually, as the land became older, these barriers in the way of the descending water would be worn away. With the formation of each mountain system, however, or with the occurrence of other accidents, such as those which are brought about by a glacial period, the paths of the streams would be disturbed, and the rivers would once again have to contend with obstructions which they seek to remove. Philosophical geographers now recognize the fact that the presence of water-falls in a country means that the topography is, in a geological sense, new; that the region has either recently been uplifted from the sea, or has, not long ago, undergone considerable revolutions, which have changed the shape of its surface.

Among the many different conditions which produce cataracts, we may note the following groups, which include the greater part of these accidents: In mountain districts small streams gathered in the tablelands or upland valleys often encounter a precipice down which they find their way in successive leaps. The cliffs over which they tumble are not, as is the case at Niagara, the product of the stream's action, but have generally been formed by a fault or a break in the rocks, the strata on one side of the disruption having been lifted so that a wall-like escarpement is created. In other cases the valley has been deeply carved by a stream of fluid or of frozen water, a river or a glacier. Water-falls of this nature, though rarely of great volume, afford the most beautiful and highest cascades in the world. Those of the Yosemite Valley, or of Lauterbrunnen, in Switzerland, are excellent examples of this kind.

Wherever a stream, be it small or great, encounters in its course conditions in which it passes from a hard to a soft rock, or rather we should say from strata which it does not easily attack to other deposits which are readily worn away, the change is commonly marked by a rapid or water-fall. This alteration may be due to any one of many causes. Commonly it is brought about by a dike, or fissure filled with volcanic rock, which lies across the channel of the river. In our limestone rocks an ancient coral reef, buried in the strata, may produce a considerable cascade. The Falls of the Ohio at Louisville are due to the fact that such an ancient reef lies athwart the path of that river.

Along the seashore wherever the waves have carved, as they often do, an overhanging steep, the streams, which may originally have flowed down gently declining beds, tumble over precipices, sometimes falling, as on the north shore of the Island of Anticosti, directly into the ocean. In all such cases we may assume that the cliffs have been driven backward into the land by the effect of the surges.

By far the commonest origin of water-falls is to be found where horizontal stratified rocks arranged in alternating beds of hard and soft character are flowed over by a considerable stream. In these conditions the bed of the river is apt to lie on one of the hard layers upon which it courses until it cuts the layer through; then encountering the underlying soft materials it quickly wears them away down to the level of the next resisting stratum, where the process is repeated, forming, it may be, a dozen steps of descent in the course of a few miles. Each of the "treads" of such a stairway is apt to be many times as wide as the fall is high; but where the river has a great volume the down rush of water is apt to break up the lower-lying harder layers so that one great fall is produced. The reader will do well to see the beautiful system of step cascades known as Trenton Falls, where West Canada Creek descends from the highland about its source through a beautiful gorge of its own carving in many successive leaps.

The foregoing brief story concerning the natural history of water-falls has led us to the point where we may begin our inquiries concerning the genesis of Niagara. This fall belongs to the last-mentioned group of cascades, that in which the course of the river is determined in a great measure by the diverse resistance which horizontically-bedded rocks opposed to the wearing action of the water. In order, however, to face the many interesting questions which this river and fall present to the naturalist, we must ask the reader at the outset to obtain a clear idea as to the conditions of the valley of the stream from the point where it leaves

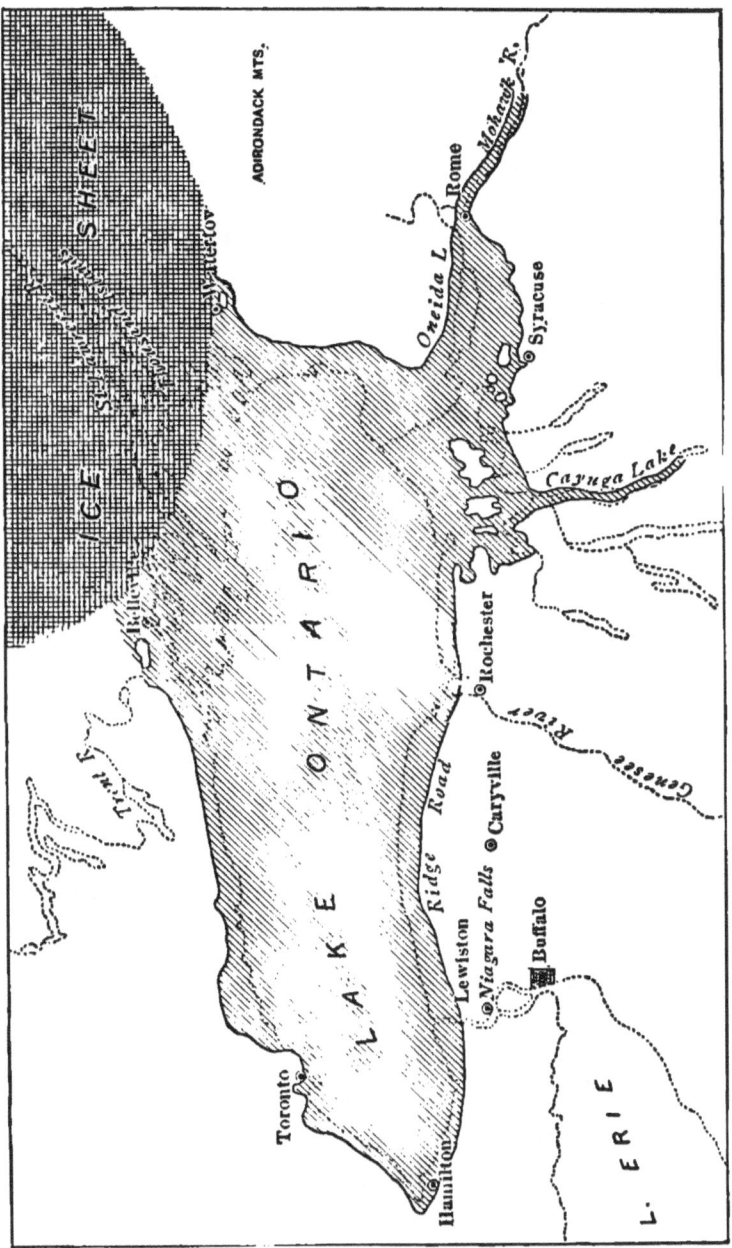

Map of Lake Iroquois.

EXPLANATION.—Modern hydrography in dotted lines. Ancient lake area shaded. Ice sheet cross-shaded.

Lake Erie to that where it enters Lake Ontario. The ideal way to obtain this impression would be to view the country from the sumit of a tower having a height of five hundred feet or more, standing at a point near the present line of the falls. It is indeed most desirable from the point of view of the teacher, as well as others who love wide views, that such a " coin of vantage " should be constructed. In passing, we may remark that such an outlook would enable the observer to command the whole field of nearly level country from lake to lake. The student would thus be able to perceive directly what he can only otherwise infer from the maps and bird's eye views. Using, however, these last named means of illustration, we readily observe the following facts concerning the course of Niagara River. We follow the prevailing fashion in terming this stream a river. It is, in fact, a mere strait connecting two fresh water seas, the one lying about three hundred feet above the other.

Near its point of exit from Lake Erie the stream passes over a low uplift of the strata which somewhat interrupts its flow. A little way on in its path the tide is divided, enclosing a large island and some smaller isles. Its movement is slow, and in general the condition of the stream and its banks remind one of the lower parts of a great river where it is about to enter the sea. The striking feature is, that from Lake Erie to Goat Island the stream has no distinct valley. It has evidently done none of that downward carving which is so conspicuous a feature in the work of all ordinary rivers where they flow at a considerable height above the ocean's level. In part this absence of a valley is to be accounted for by the absolute purity of the water. Ordinary rivers bear much sediment, the coarser parts of which are driven along the bottom continuously, though slightly wearing the bed-rock away as they rub over it; but in the Niagara all these sediments which the streams bring from the uplands are deposited in the chain of the great lakes.

At Goat Island the conditions are suddenly changed. In the rapids and in the main falls the river descends about two hundred feet into a deep gorge, through which it flows as far as Lewiston in a more or less tumultuous manner. At this point the channel passes through the escarpement which borders the southern margin of Lake Ontario. Here it ceases to flow as rapidly as before, the tide of waters finding ample room in the deep channel for a leisurely journey to the lower lake.

The gorge of the Niagara, though deep, is very narrow: to the eye of the trained observer it appears almost as unlike an ordinary river valley as is the path of the stream above the cataract. Everywhere the walls are steep; there is no trace of the alluvial plain which normally borders great rivers; nor do we find the slope of country towards the edge of the cliff which is so characteristic of ordinary valleys. This depression, indeed, is a true cañon, a trough carved by a main stream without any coincident work of erosion effected by the rain, frost and water-courses operating on either side of its path. These features have led geologists, as they well may lead any intelligent observer, to the conclusion that the Niagara River is from beginning to end a new-made stream; a watercourse which originated not as most of our American rivers have in remote ages, but in the geological yesterday. The reason for this sudden coming into existence of the Niagara, the steps which led to its invention, are now undergoing a very careful discussion through the labors of several able geologists.* Although there is much which is still doubtful concerning the history of this singular stream, a great deal of interest has been well ascertained. The outlines of this matter we will now endeavor to set before the reader.

In endeavoring to comprehend the history of Niagara, it is necessary to take account of the singular conditions presented by the great valley in which it lies. The St. Lawrence is on some accounts the most curious of all the great vales which geographers have had an opportunity to study. The most of the river-

---

*The literature concerning the problems of the Niagara River is abundant, but widely scattered. The ablest single contribution to the subject is by Mr. G. K. Gilbert, Geologist, U. S. Geological survey. It is contained in the sixth annual report of the Commissioners of the State reservation at Niagara, for the year 1889.—Albany, James B. Lyon, Printer, 1890. References to various other treatises on the subject may be found in the foot-note of that paper.

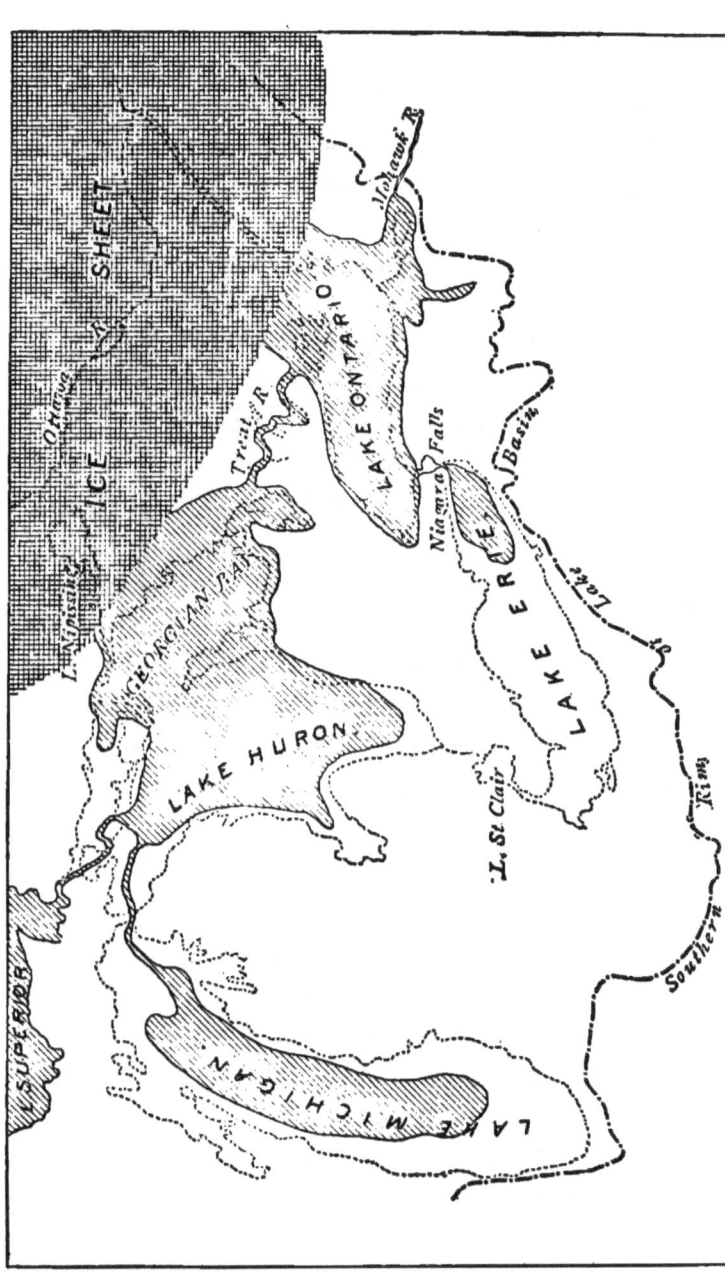

Hypothetic hydrography at a date before the melting of the great glacier from the St. Lawrence Valley.

EXPLANATION.—Water-parting in heavy broken line. Modern hydrography in light broken lines. Ancient rivers in full lines. Ancient lakes shaded. Ice sheet cross-shaded.

basins in the world have their boundaries defined by a considerable elevation. If, here and there, they have a low side over which we may pass to a neighboring valley without traversing a decided water-shed, the partial breach of the boundaries is very limited in its length. In the St. Lawrence valley, however, from the lower end of Lake Ontario to the mouth of Lake Superior the basin is on its southern side but ill-defined.

The low, broad ridge which separates the drainage from that of the streams which flow into the Hudson, or into the Mississippi, is frequently breached by depressions through which the waters belonging to the Great Lakes system may readily be discharged whenever their elevation is considerably altered, or when by chance a barrier is interposed to their exit through the Gulf of St. Lawrence. Accidents of this description have been probably of frequent occurrence, so that from time to time the geographical relations of these waters have been greatly changed.

The Great Lakes of the St. Lawrence valley were probably in existence before the last glacial period, though they were doubtless extended and somewhat modified in form by the wearing of the rocks which occurred in that wonderful age. With the beginning of the glacial period the ice-sheet of eastern North America, which is now limited to Greenland, rapidly extended its bounds over the land to the northward of the Great Lakes. It soon filled their basins, and extended southward until its margin attained the Ohio River where Cincinnati now stands, and lay over the head-waters of all the valleys of the streams which pour from the South into the Great Lakes. It is easy to see that such an ice-sheet having the depth of a mile or more would profoundly disturb the drainage of these rivers. In its advance it would first create a dam across the waters of the St. Lawrence River, compelling the lakes to rise until they discharged through some of the low places on their southern boundary ; next it must have filled their basins with ice, and deepened the sheet until its surface lay thousands of feet above their floor. We cannot trace the history of these alterations which the advance of the glacial envelope brought upon this field of land and water. But the steps in the alterations may be inferred from what happened when the envelope retreated stage by stage until it vanished from the continent, or at least from the part of the field with which we are concerned. For a time the barrier lay in such a position that the waters of the Lakes below Superior were barred out from the passage of Niagara, flowing over into the valley of the Ohio through a channel passing by the site of the City of Fort Wayne, and thence into the Wabash River. This old waterway has been preserved with unmistakable clearness. With the further retreat of the ice-front to the northeastward, the line of the barrier was withdrawn to near the present mouth of Lake

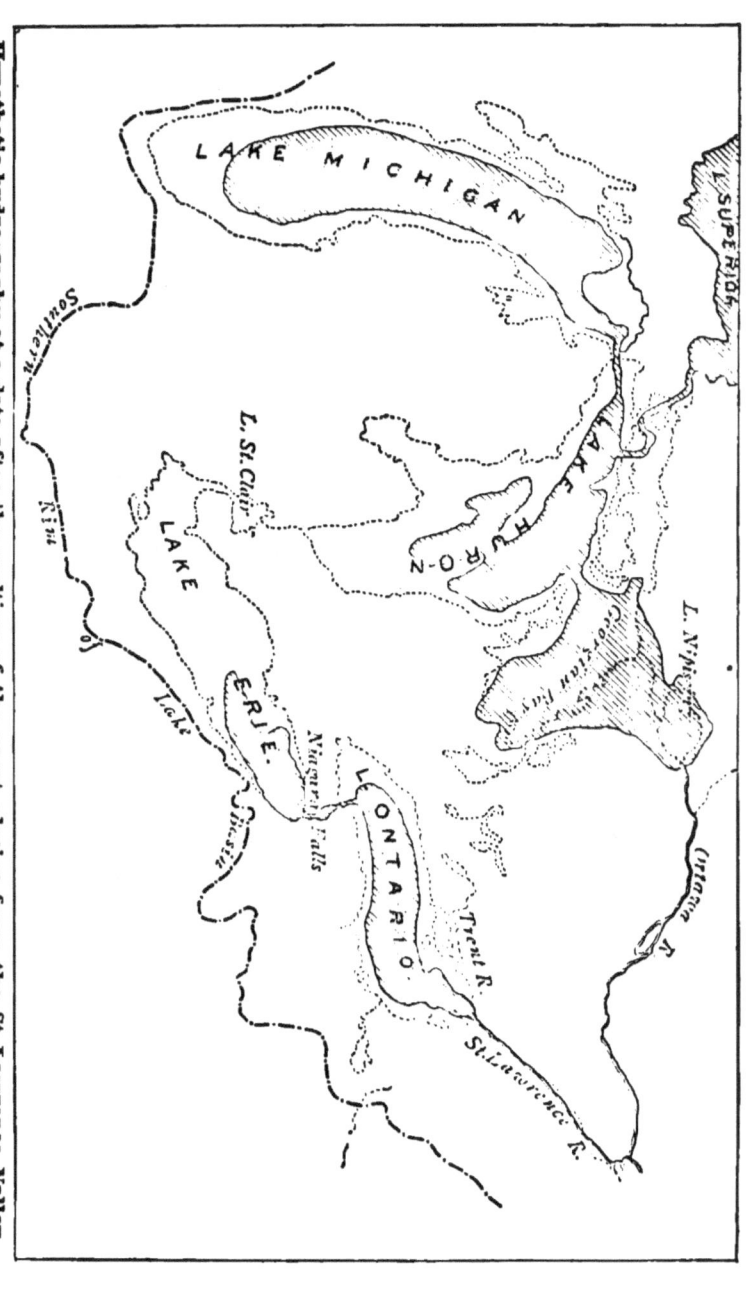

Hypothetic hydrography at a date after the melting of the great glacier from the St. Lawrence Valley.

EXPLANATION.—Water-parting in heavy broken line. Modern hydrography in light broken lines. Ancient rivers in full lines. Ancient lakes shaded.

Ontario, where it flows into the St. Lawrence River. At this time the level of the Great Lakes was lowered by successive stages, though on the whole rather suddenly, to the amount of five hundred and fifty feet.

With the last mentioned condition of the ice barrier the exit of the Great Lakes changed to a path which led through Central New York, down the valley of the Mohawk River. The channel still shows the marks of the great tide of water, probably as great in its volume as that which now passes Niagara Falls. Those who journey by the New York Central Railway to and from Albany, may note at Little Falls the broad gorge of the sometime great river which is now occupied by a relatively small stream. It might be supposed that at this stage the observer would have found the Niagara river flowing in somewhere near its present position. But here comes in one of the extraordinary accidents of that period of geographic wonders, the great Ice Age. When the ice lay over the country to the north of the Great Lakes, the part of the continent which it occupied appears to have been borne down by the weight of the mass in such a manner that it sloped to the northward at the rate of two or three feet to the mile. The result was that the basin of Lake Erie was to a great extent dry, and that of Lake Huron did not connect across to the southward through Lake St. Clair, but through Georgian Bay, and thence by a channel occupying the site of the

Trent River to the northern part of Lake Ontario. At a yet later stage, when the ice barrier was still further withdrawn, so that the channel of the St. Lawrence was open, another channel was found by way of the Ottawa River, so that the upper lakes no longer emptied by way of Lake Ontario.

After the ice passed completely away from this part of the country, the land recovered from its southward down-tilting, Lake Erie regained its waters, and the tide from Lakes Michigan and Huron began to flow, as at present, by way of the Detroit River and Lake St. Clair. This was probably the age when the present Niagara River came into existence. We have already noted the fact that as a whole the valley of the Niagara, both above and below the falls, appears to be a piece of stream-carving done in very modern times. Although it doubtless antedates the earliest chapters of human history of which we have any written records, it almost certainly is newer than the records of man which we find written in certain ancient art remains, such as those which were found with the Calaveras skull in California. The stream may have begun its work not more than ten thousand years ago. It appears, however, that there was a pre-glacial Niagara.

If the reader will go to the cliff which borders the lowland along the lake, a precipice carved at some period when Lake Ontario was higher than at present, and walk westward from the river, he will observe that at the town of St. David's, a few miles west of Queenston, the cliffs turn inland in a way which indicates that here of old was a valley through which a great river found its way to the lake. Going southward to the site of the whirlpool we find there a point where, and where alone, the steep rocky walls of the Niagara cañon fail, and their place is taken by heaps of drift material, evidently brought to its present site by the ice of the glacial time which here, as in many other regions, filled the pre-glacial valleys with detritus. In the opinion of those who have most attentively studied the problem, there was an old Niagara River extending a part of its channel from St. David's to the whirlpool, and probably from that point along much the same line as the present stream toward the existing falls. It is possible, however, that this old channel may have bent away to the west from the whirlpool, and attained Lake Erie at some unknown point. If the old channel entered the present Niagara gorge at the pool we have to assume that when the stream, long dispossessed by the glacier, was permitted again to flow, it found the channel to St. David's so completely filled that it was easier to plunge over the Queenston bluff at a new point, and thence in the retreat of the falls to carve the cañon back to its present site. It may be that a part of the channel above the enlargement at the whirlpool was also carved in the old pre-glacial days, filled in with glacial waste, and afterwards swept clear of the obstruction by the mighty stream.

To the reader who has paid no attention to the geographic changes which were produced in the last ice time, such alterations in the path of a river may seem most improbable. The geologist, however, knows that these have been among the commoner incidents in this chapter of the earth's history. Hardly any of the considerable streams which existed within the glaciated field before the advent of the ice escaped such perturbation. We could in an *a priore* way predict that a stream lying in the position of the Niagara River, where the amount of glacial waste deposited on the surface was very great, would be so far effaced by detritus that when the tide again began to flow, a portion at least of its channel would depart from its primitive position. In fact, among the many detailed inquiries which the geologist has a chance to make in the old glacial fields there are few which are more interesting and, indeed, more perplexing than these which concern the relation of the ancient and existing river valleys.

From this general and rather wide consideration of the Niagara problem, which has brought us in face of some of the majestic actions of the past, we may now profitably turn to the detailed phenomena exhibited in the Falls and in the gorge between them and Queenston. The student will do well to begin these inquiries by a journey to the Cave of the Winds, where, penetrating behind a thin strip of the falling water, he can see something of the condition of the steep over which the cataract plunges. He should also observe the rocks in the faces of the cliffs below the Falls. He will readily note the fact that the top of the precipice is occupied by a somewhat massive limestone. This rock is, it is true, divided by joints into large blocks, but these are hard, and are not much worn by the clean water which at the margin of the escarpment shoots clear of their face in the manner shown by the diagram. Below this limestone, which is extensively developed in New York and in the adjacent parts of the continent, and which most properly bears the name of " Niagara Limestone," there is a less considerable thickness of thin-layered shaley beds known as the " Niagara Shale." Yet below lie beds of the Clinton Age, composed of somewhat coherent limestone shales sandstones. . At the base of the section of the Falls and steep, occupying more than half of its height, are the beds of the Medina formation, mostly made up of rather frail sandstones and thin reddish shaley layers. From what the reader can see in the Cave of the Winds, and what he can readily infer by observing the rocks bared in the cliffs near the Falls, he will readily understand that the Niagara Limestone is the rock which takes the brunt of the work required in maintaining the precipice, down which its river plunges. He will see also that this hard edge of the cliff projects beyond its base, thus giving free room for the fall to descend unbroken to the level of the stream

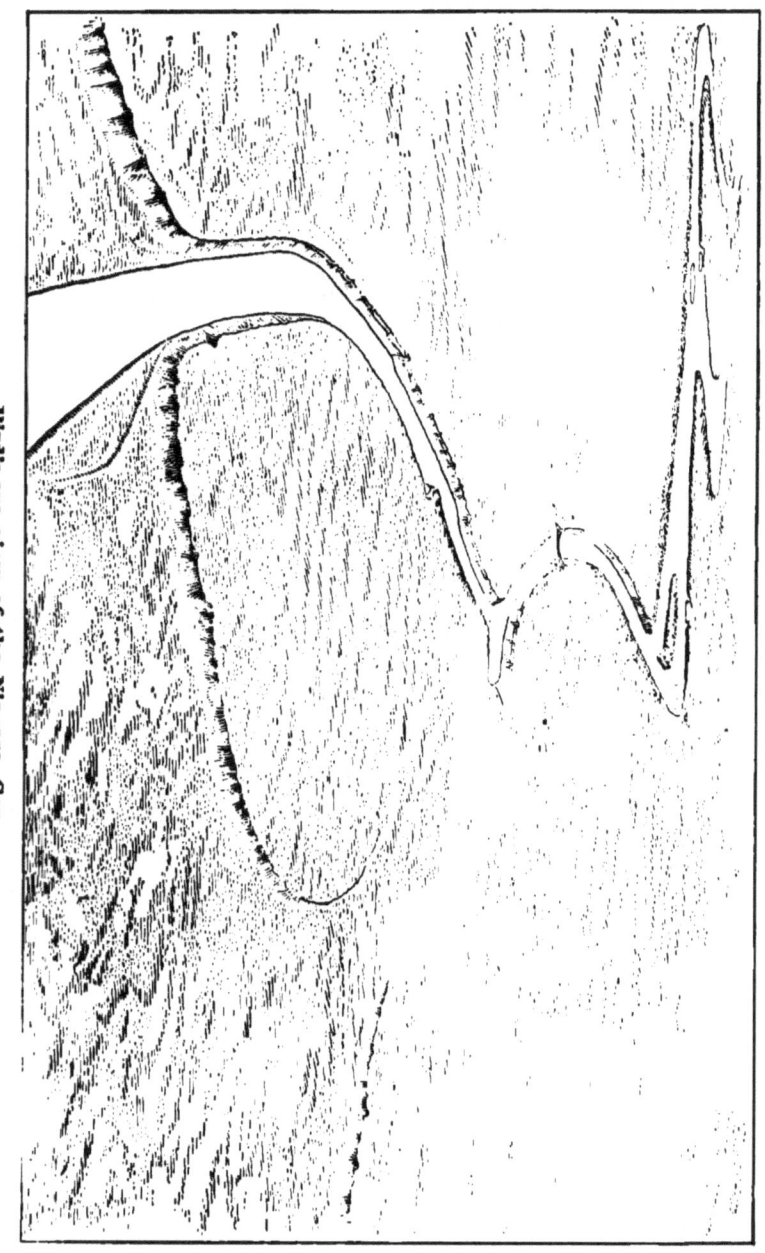

Bird's-eye view of the Niagara Gorge.

below, and thence downward in the tumult of waters to the river bed to a greater depth than the visible face of the Falls.

From time to time as abundant general observations and accurate surveys show, the Niagara cornice of the wall is so far left unsupported by the more rapid wearing of the lower-lying softer beds that it breaks down by its own weight and falls in ruins to the base of the submerged cliff at the foot of the cascade. In this position we cannot see what becomes of the debris, but from what we may readily observe at other points we can make some interesting and trustworthy inferences. Along many rivers the student of such phenomena can find places where ancient cataracts have left their bases bare by the shrinkage or diversion of the streams which produced them; thus at Little Falls on the Mohawk, which, as before noted, was once the path of exit of the Great Lake waters, there was in the olden day a great cataract, the most of which is now above the level of the shrunken river. Here we find the rocks once trodden by the fall excavated in great well-like "pot-holes," some of which are ten feet or more in diameter, and with more than that depth. Each of these cavities has evidently been carved out by the bits of hard rock which the stream brought into them, the fragments having been made to journey round and round in a circle, forming what is often a dome-shaped chamber, widening toward its base. Such whirling movements of water may be observed in a miniature way where a stream from a hydrant falls into a basin. The base of the Niagara cliff is doubtless under-cut in the manner above described, the graving tools being the hard fragments which fall from its upper parts.

As we may behold in the Cave of the Winds, the whirlings of the water-laden air and jets of spray tend somewhat to soften and dissolve the layers of the shale, and thus to bring about that recession of the face which causes the limestone to jut beyond the base of the precipice. Beneath the level of the stream the violent swayings of the tormented water, beaten by the strokes of the Falls, doubtless serve yet more effectively to erode the soft rocks of the Medina formations. These actions co-operating with the pot-holing work keep the cliff ever retreating at its base at a little greater rate than at its summit, the limestone capstone falling only when the excavation beneath denies it effective support. In the above described features Niagara Falls are in no sense peculiar. There are probably within two hundred miles of their site over fifty cascades which have been engendered and maintained by the same simple conditions of an upper hard layer and lower-lying more easily worn strata. It should be remarked, however, that the greater the height down which the plunge of water takes place, and the larger its volume, the more vigorous is the assault upon the base of the cliff through the development of pot-hole excavations and the lashing which the troubled waters apply to the rocks. But for the fact that the tide of Niagara, though of vast volume, is perfectly clean, the retreat of the Falls precipice towards Lake Erie would have been far more rapid than under the existing conditions. If, in place of the marvelously pure lake water the turbid stream of the Mississippi poured down this steep, the scouring action of the tumult beneath the fall would produce a vast increase of erosion. In these assumed conditions it might well be that the observer would find some sorry remnant of this great cascade far to the southward of its present position, perhaps within the limits of what is now Lake Erie. The difference in the effect of pure and turbid water, when forced against hard rocks may be judged by the fact that while a glass window may be washed with a hydrant stream for an indefinite period without mark of abrasion, a similar stream of very turbid water will in a short time bring about a noticeable scratching of the glass.

We are now in a position to understand how it is that the Falls have cut their way back through the great distance which separates them from the Queenston bluff over which the river flowed when it was first made free to follow its present course. It is a fine tour of the imagination to conceive how in some day after the ice age, when the country had assumed the elevation and attitude which required the development of the second Niagara river, the waters broke over the barrier near Buffalo, sweeping across the gently sloping country to the Queenston cliffs, there plunging down in what was at first a broken cataract rather than a fall, into the lowlands about Ontario, or it may have been directly into the waters of the lake, then more elevated than now. Very quickly the undercutting process above described must have converted the cataract into a vertical fall. In a few score years the process of retreat of the steep over which the water fell must have begun the excavation of the great gorge. It may help the reader to conceive the advance of the process to imagine a great auger boring away upon some soft material, the tool while turning being drawn slowly across the surface. In the similitude, the whirling waters at the base of the cascade with their armament of stones, represents the auger, and the wide field of strata which have been carved the material which is bored by the moving tool.

For many years geologists, who are ever trying to measure the duration of the past, have endeavored to compute the time which has elapsed since the excavation of the gorge below Niagara Falls began. It seemed at first likely that the time occupied in this great work might be reckoned in a somewhat definite way. Long ago it became evident that the Falls were slowly advancing up the river through the undermin-

RIVER

NIAGARA LIMESTONE

NIAGARA SHALE

CLINTON FORMATION

MEDINA FORMATION

Section of Niagara Falls, showing the arrangement of hard and soft strata, and illustrating a theory of the process of erosion.

ing of their base and the consequent crumbling of the overhanging limestone at the foot of the precipice. In 1842, Dr. James Hall made a careful map showing the position of the different parts of the Falls, which were referred to monuments from which subsequent surveys could do work that would afford a basis for comparisons. A third of a century later another survey was made by officers of the U. S. Engineers. In 1886 Mr. R. S. Woodward made yet another careful map of the region. It now appears, however, according to Mr. G. K. Gilbert, that one or more of these delineations is somewhat in error, for at certain places the outline of the front projects beyond the position indicated by Hall's survey. After a careful consideration of these discrepancies, Mr. Gilbert says: "Nevertheless a critical study, not merely of the bare lines on the chart, but also of the fuller data in the surveyor's notes, leads to the belief that the rate of recession in the central part of the Horseshoe Fall is approximately determined, and that it is somewhere between four feet and six feet per annum. The amount of falling away at the sides of the Horseshoe is not well determined, but this is of less importance, for such falling away effects the width of the gorge rather than its length, and it is the length with which we are concerned."

If we could assume that all the cutting of the gorge from the Falls to Queenston had been done since the stage in the retreat of the ice sheet when the river, as we now know it, began to flow, it would seem to be an easy matter to make an approximate computation as to the length of time which had been required to effect the task. As yet, however, we must hesitate to make an assertion, and, following the example of Mr. Gilbert, regard the problem as one which demands a far more careful study than it has as yet received before a judgment can properly be given. It is in a high degree improbable that the rate of retreat in the last forty years is anywhere near an average of the movement since the excavation of the cañon began. Between the Falls and Queenston the rocks which have been cut through, though of a tolerably uniform nature, have here and there local peculiarities which may have greatly accelerated the rate at which the Falls have worked upstream. The height of the Falls has altered in this movement, and it is very probable that the volume of water may have been subjected to considerable changes through the alterations of climate which have attended the passing away of the glacial sheet. In addition to these evident sources of error there are others connected with the irregular tilting movements of this part of the continent which, as before noticed, have perturbed the drainage since the close of the time when the ice sheet lay over the basin of the St. Lawrence.

At present it is tolerably safe to reckon the rate of retreat of Niagara Falls at about five hundred feet in a century. The reader may, if he pleases, assume that this is a fair measure of the speed with which the cascade has worked back from the Queenston escarpment; but if he makes the computation he should regard it as amusing rather than instructive work. It is evident, however, that in the course of a thousand years the Fall is likely to be about a mile nearer Lake Erie than it is at present.

It is most probable that long before this planet has dispensed with the presence of man, and before any geological or geographical changes have effaced this land, the question will have to be met whether our successors shall permit the recession of the Falls to bring about the draining of Lake Erie and the adjacent waters. In the illumination of that time, indeed we may say in the light of our own, it will not appear difficult to arrest this natural development by which the recession of the cascade tends to drain away the lake from which its waters flow. New channels can be excavated which will divert the stream to some point on the line of the cañon where a fresh field of excavation can be provided for the cataract; or if it seems worth while, an excavation can be made beneath the stream at a point above the Falls, and a hard masonry support provided for the Niagara limestone, which, as we have noted, forms the cornice over which the water plunges.

If we may judge the motives of the future by those of the present, the decision as to the eventual fate of Niagara will rest upon economic considerations. Such considerations, indeed, are likely in course of time, and that not long, to lead to the utilization of the vast amount of power which now goes to waste at this point. So long as the factory had to be placed near its water-wheel the demand for the energy of the Falls was not very insistent. If, however, as seems most likely, electricians devise means whereby the tide of force made available by this leap of waters can be carried, without too much loss, to points five hundred miles or more away, we may find New York and Chicago, and a hundred other places, asking for a share of the energy which here goes to waste. It is indeed most likely that the arrest in the southward march of Niagara will be brought about by the diversion of its waters to the turbines which drive dynamos.

The foregoing considerations may make it evident to the reader that Niagara Falls should not be viewed as a mere spectacle. They should be taken as majestic natural phenomena which throw light on many important chapters in the history of our continent. It is indeed doubtful if at any other place in the world the mind stimulated by a majestic scene is so naturally led to inquiries full of learned as well as of human interest.

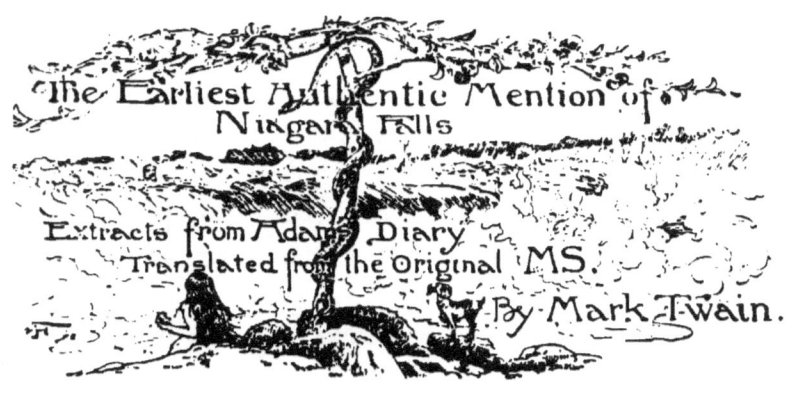

The Earliest Authentic Mention of Niagara Falls

Extracts from Adam's Diary
Translated from the Original MS.
By Mark Twain.

MONDAY.—This new creature with the long hair is a good deal in the way. It is always hanging around and following me about. I don't like this; I am not used to company. I wish it would stay with the other animals. . . . . Cloudy to-day, wind in the east; think we shall have rain. . . . . *We?* Where did I get that word? . . . . I remember now,—the new creature uses it.

TUESDAY.—Been examining the great waterfall. It is the finest thing on the estate, I think. The new creature calls it Niagara Falls—why, I am sure I do not know. Says it *looks* like Niagara Falls. That is not a reason, it is mere waywardness and imbecility. I get no chance to name anything myself. The new creature names everything that comes along, before I can get in a protest. And always that same pretext is offered—it *looks* like the thing. There is the dodo, for instance. Says the moment one looks at it one sees at a glance that it " looks like a dodo." It will have to keep that name, no doubt. It wearies me to fret about it, but it does no good, anyway. Dodo! It looks no more like a dodo than I do.

WEDNESDAY.—Built me a shelter against the rain, but could not have it to myself in peace. The new creature intruded. When I tried to put it out it shed water out of the holes it looks with, and wiped it away with the back of its paws, and made a noise such as some of the other animals make when they are in distress. I wish it would not talk; it is always talking. That sounds like a cheap fling at the poor creature, a slur; but I do not mean it so. I have never heard the human voice before, and any new and strange sound intruding itself here upon the solemn hush of these dreaming solitudes offends my ear and seems a false note. And this new sound is so close to me; it is right at my shoulder, right at my ear, first on one side and then on the other, and I am used only to sounds that are more or less distant from me.

FRIDAY.—The naming goes recklessly on, in spite of anything I can do. I had a very good name for the estate, and it was musical and pretty—GARDEN-OF-EDEN. Privately, I continue to call it that, but not any longer publicly. The new creature says it is all woods and rocks and scenery, and therefore has no resemblance to a garden. Says it *looks* like a park, and does not look like anything *but* a park. Consequently, without consulting me it has been new named—NIAGARA FALLS PARK. This is sufficiently high-handed, it seems to me. And already there is a sign up:

> KEEP OFF
> THE GRASS.

My life is not as happy as it was.

SATURDAY.—The new creature eats too much fruit. We are going to run short, most likely. "We" again—that is *its* word; mine, too, now, from hearing it so much. Good deal of fog this morning. I do not go out in the fog, myself. The new creature does. It goes out in all weathers, and stumps right in with its muddy feet. And talks. It used to be so pleasant and quiet here.

SUNDAY.—Pulled through. This day is getting to be more and more trying. It was selected and set apart last November as a day of rest. I already had six of them per week before. This is another of those unaccountable things. There seems to be too much legislation, too much fussing, and fixing, and tidying-up, and not enough of the better-let-well-enough-alone policy. [*Mem.*—Must keep that sort of opinions to myself.] This morning found the new creature trying to clod apples out of that forbidden tree.

MONDAY.—The new creature says its name is Eve. That is all right, I have no objections. Says it is to call it by when I want it to come. I said it was superfluous, then. The word evidently raised me in its respect; and indeed it is a large, good word and will bear repetition. It says it is not an It, it is a She. This is probably doubtful; yet it is all one to me; what she is were nothing to me if she would but go by herself and not talk.

TUESDAY.—She has littered the whole estate with execrable names and offensive signs:

☞ THIS WAY TO THE WHIRLPOOL.

☞ THIS WAY TO GOAT ISLAND.

☞ CAVE OF THE WINDS THIS WAY.

She says this park would make a tidy summer resort, if there were any custom for it. Summer resort—another invention of hers—just words, without any meaning. What is a summer resort? But it is best not to ask her, she has such a rage for explaining.

FRIDAY.—She has taken to begging and imploring me to stop going over the Falls. What harm does it do? Says it makes her shudder. I wonder why; I have always done it—always liked the plunge, and the excitement and the coolness. I supposed it was what the Falls were for. They have no other use that I can see, and they must have been made for something. She says they were only made for scenery—like the rhinoceros and the mastodon.

I went over the Falls in a barrel—not satisfactory to her. Went over in a tub—still not satisfactory. Swam the Whirlpool and the Rapids in a fig-leaf suit. It got much damaged. Hence, tedious complaints about my extravagance. I am too much hampered here. What I need is change of scene.

SATURDAY.—I escaped last Tuesday night, and traveled two days, and built me another shelter, in a secluded place, and obliterated my tracks as well as I could, but she hunted me out by means of a beast which she has tamed and calls a wolf, and came making that pitiful noise again, and shedding that water out of the places she looks with. I was obliged to return with her, but will presently emigrate again, when occasion offers. She engages herself in many foolish things: among others, trying to study out why the animals called lions and tigers live on grass and flowers, when, as she says, the sort of teeth they wear would indicate that they were intended to eat each other. This is foolish, because to do that would be to kill each other, and that would introduce what, as I understand it, is called " death "; and death, as I have been told, has not yet entered the Park. Which is a pity, on some accounts.

SUNDAY.—Pulled through.

MONDAY.—I believe I see what the week is for: it is to give time to rest up from the weariness of Sunday. It seems a good idea, in a region where good ideas are rather conspicuously scarce. [*Mem.*—Must keep this sort of remarks private.] .... She has been climbing that tree again. Clodded her out of it. She said nobody was looking. Seems to consider that a sufficient justification for chancing any dangerous thing. Told her that. The word justification moved her admiration—and envy, too, I thought. It is a good word.

THURSDAY.—She told me she was made out of a rib taken from my body. This is at least doubtful, if not more than that. I have not missed any rib. . . . She is in much trouble about the buzzard; says grass does not agree with it; is afraid she can't raise it; thinks it was intended to live on decayed flesh. The buzzard must get along the best it can with what is provided. We cannot overturn the whole scheme to accommodate the buzzard.

SATURDAY.—She fell in the pond yesterday, when she was looking at herself in it, which she is always doing. She nearly strangled, and said it was most uncomfortable. This made her sorry for the creatures which live in there, which she calls fish, for she continues to fasten names on to things that don't need them and don't come when they are called by them, which is a matter of no consequence to her, she is such a fool anyway; so she got a lot of them out and brought them in and put them in my bed to keep warm, but I have noticed them now and then all day

The Horse-Shoe Falls from Goat Island.

and I don't see that they are any happier there than they were before. When night comes I shall throw them outdoors. I will not sleep with them, for I find them clammy and unpleasant to lie among when a person hasn't anything on.

SUNDAY.—Pulled through.

TUESDAY.—She has taken up with a snake now. The other animals are glad, for she was always experimenting with them and bothering them; and I am glad, because the snake talks, and this enables me to get a rest.

FRIDAY.—She says the snake advises her to try the fruit of that tree, and says the result will be a great and fine and noble education. I told her there would be another result, too—it would introduce death into the world. That was a mistake—it had been better to keep the remark to myself; it only gave her an idea —she could save the sick buzzard, and furnish fresh meat to the despondent lions and tigers. I advised her to keep away from the tree. She said she wouldn't. I foresee trouble. Will emigrate.

WEDNESDAY.—I have had a variegated time. I escaped that night, and rode a horse all night as fast as he could go, hoping to get clear out of the Garden and hide in some other country before the trouble should begin; but it was not to be. About an hour after sun-up, as I was riding through a flowery plain where thousands of animals were grazing, slumbering, or playing with each other, according to their common wont, all of a sudden they broke into a tempest of frightful noises, and in one moment the plain was a frantic commotion and every beast was destroying its neighbor. I knew what it meant—Eve had eaten that fruit, and death was come into the world. . . . . The tigers ate my horse, paying no attention when I ordered them to desist, and they would even have eaten me if I had stayed—which I didn't, but went away in much haste. . . . . I found this place, outside the Garden, and was fairly comfortable for a few days, but she has found me out. Found me out, and has named the place Tonawanda—says it *looks* like that. In fact I was not sorry she came, for there are but meagre pickings here, and she brought some of those apples. I was obliged to eat them, I was so hungry. It was against my principles, but I find that principles have no real force except when one is well fed. . . . She came curtained in boughs and bunches of leaves, and when I asked her what she meant by such nonsense, and snatched them away and threw them down, she tittered and blushed. I had never seen a person titter and blush before, and to me it seemed unbecoming and idiotic. She said I would soon know how it was myself. This was correct. Hungry as I was, I laid down the apple half eaten—certainly the best one I ever saw, considering the lateness of the season—and arrayed myself in the discarded boughs and branches, and then spoke to her with some severity and ordered her to go and get some more and not make such a spectacle of herself. She did it, and after this we crept down to where the wild-beast battle had been, and collected some skins, and I made her patch together a couple of suits proper for public occasions. They are uncomfortable, it is true, but stylish, and that is the main point about clothes. . . . I find she is a good deal of a companion. I see I should be lonesome and depressed without her, now that I have lost my property. Another thing, she says it is ordered that we work for our living hereafter. She will be useful. I will superintend.

TEN DAYS LATER.—She accuses *me* of being the cause of our disaster! She says, with apparent sincerity and truth, that the Serpent assured her that the forbidden fruit was not apples, it was chestnuts. I said I was innocent, then, for I had not eaten any chestnuts. She said the Serpent informed her that "chestnut" was a figurative term meaning an aged and mouldy joke. I turned pale at that, for I have made many jokes to pass the weary time, and some of them could have been of that sort, though I had honestly supposed they were new when I made them. She asked me if I had made one just at the time of the catastrophe. I was obliged to admit that I had made one to myself, though not aloud. It was this. I was thinking about the Falls, and I said to myself, "How wonderful it is to see that vast body of water tumble down there!" Then in an instant a bright thought flashed into my head, and I let it fly, saying, " It would be a deal more wonderful to see it tumble *up* there!"—and I was just about to kill myself with laughing at it when all nature broke loose in war and death and I had to flee for my life. " There," she said, with triumph, " that is just it; the Serpent mentioned that very jest, and called it the First Chestnut, and said it was coeval with the creation." Alas, I am indeed to blame. Would that I were not witty; oh, would that I had never had that radiant thought!

NEXT YEAR.—We have named it Cain. She caught it while I was up country trapping on the North Shore of the Erie; caught it in the timber a couple of miles from our dug-out—or it might have been four, she isn't certain which. It resembles us in some ways, and may be a relation. That is what she thinks, but this is an error, in my judgment. The difference in size warrants the conclusion that it is a different and new kind of animal—a fish, perhaps, though when I put it in the water to see, it sank, and she plunged in and snatched it out before there was opportunity for the experiment to determine the matter. I still think it is a fish, but she is indifferent about what it is, and will not let me have it to try. I do not understand this. The coming of the creature seems to have changed her whole nature and made her unreasonable about experiments. She thinks more of it than she does of any of the other animals, but is not able to explain why. Her mind is disordered—everything shows it. Sometimes she carries the fish in her arms half the night when it complains and wants to get to the water. At such times the water comes out of the places in her face that she looks out of, and she pats the fish on the back and makes soft sounds with her mouth to soothe it, and betrays sorrow and solicitude in a hundred ways. I have never seen her do like this with any other fish, and it troubles me greatly. She used to carry the young tigers around so, and play with them, before we lost our property, but it was only play; she never took on about them like this when their dinner disagreed with them.

SUNDAY.—She don't work, Sundays, but lies around all tired out, and likes to have the fish wallow over her; and she makes fool noises to amuse it, and pretends to chew its paws, and that makes it laugh. I have not seen a fish before that could laugh. This makes me doubt . . . . I have come to like Sunday myself. Superintending all the week tires a body so. There ought to be more Sundays. In the old days they were tough, but now they come handy.

WEDNESDAY.—It isn't a fish. I cannot quite make out what it is. It makes curious devilish noises when not satisfied, and says "goo-goo" when it is. It is not one of us, for it doesn't walk; it is not a bird, for it doesn't fly; it is not a frog, for it doesn't hop; it is not a snake, for it doesn't crawl; I feel sure it is not a fish, though I cannot get a chance to find out whether it can swim or not. It merely lies around, and mostly on its back, with its feet up. I have not seen any other animal do that before. I said I believed it was an enigma; but she only admired the word without understanding it. In my judgment it is either an enigma or some kind of a bug. If it dies, I will take it apart and see what its arrangements are. I never had a thing perplex me so.

THREE MONTHS LATER.—The perplexity merely augments instead of diminishing. I sleep but little. It has ceased from lying around, and goes about on its four legs, now. Yet it differs from the other four-legged animals, in that its front legs are unusually short, consequently this causes the main part of its person to stick up uncomfortably high in the air, and this is not attractive. It is built much as we are, but its method of traveling shows that it is not of our breed. The short front legs and long hind ones indicate that it is of the kangaroo family, but it is a marked variation of the species, since the true kangaroo hops, whereas this one never does. Still it is a curious and interesting variety, and has not been catalogued before. As I discovered it, I have felt justified in securing the credit of the discovery by attaching my name to it, and hence have called it *Kangaroorum Adam-*

iensis. .... It must have been a young one when it came, for it has grown exceedingly since. It must be five times as big, now, as it was then, and when discontented is able to make from twenty-two to thirty-eight times the noise it made at first. Coercion does not modify this, but has the contrary effect. For this reason I discontinued the system. She reconciles it by persuasion, and by giving it things which she had told it she wouldn't give it before. As observed previously, I was not at home when it first came, and she told me she found it in the woods. It seems odd that it should be the only one, yet it must be so, for I have worn myself out these many weeks trying to find another one to add to my collection, and for this one to play with; for surely then it would be quieter and we could tame it more easily. But I find none, nor any vestige of any; and strangest of all, no tracks. It has to live on the ground, it cannot help itself; therefore, how does it get about without leaving a track? I have set a dozen traps, but they do no good. I catch all small animals except that one; animals that merely go into the trap out of curiosity, I think, to see what the milk is there for. They never drink it.

THREE MONTHS LATER.—The Kangaroo still continues to grow, which is very strange and perplexing. I never knew one to be so long getting its growth. It has fur on its head now; not like kangaroo fur, but exactly like our hair except that it is much finer and softer, and instead of being black is red. I am like to lose my mind over the capricious and harassing developments of this unclassifiable zoological freak. If I could catch another one—but that is hopeless ; it is a new variety, and the only sample ; this is plain. But I caught a true kangaroo and brought it in, thinking that this one, being lonesome, would rather have that for company than have no kin at all, or any animal it could feel a nearness to or get sympathy from in its forlorn condition here among strangers who do not know its ways or habits, or what to do to make it feel that it is among friends ; but it was a mistake—it went into such fits at the sight of the kangaroo that I was convinced it had never seen one before. I pity the poor noisy little animal, but there is nothing I can do to make it happy. If I could tame it—but that is out of the question ; the more I try the worse I seem to make it. It grieves me to the heart to see it in its little storms of sorrow and passion. I wanted to let it go, but she wouldn't hear of it. That seemed cruel and not like her ; and yet she may be right. It might be lonelier than ever ; for since I cannot find another one, how could *it?*

FIVE MONTHS LATER.—It is not a kangaroo. No, for it supports itself by holding to her finger, and thus goes a few steps on its hind legs, and then falls down. It is probably some kind of a bear ; and yet it has no tail—as yet—and no fur, except on its head.

It still keeps on growing—that is a curious circumstance, for bears get their growth earlier than this. Bears are dangerous—since our catastrophe—and I shall not be satisfied to have this one prowling about the place much longer without a muzzle on. I have offered to get her a kangaroo if she would let this one go, but it did no good—she is determined to run us into all sorts of foolish risks, I think. She was not like this before she lost her mind.

A FORTNIGHT LATER.—I examined its mouth. There is no danger yet; it has only one tooth. It has no tail yet. It makes more noise now than it ever did before—and mainly at night. I have moved out. But I shall go over, mornings, to breakfast, and to see if it has more teeth. If it gets a mouthful of teeth it will be time for it to go, tail or no tail, for a bear does not need a tail in order to be dangerous.

FOUR MONTHS LATER.—I have been off hunting and fishing a month, up in the region that she calls Buffalo; I don't know why, unless it is because there are not any buffalos there. Meantime the bear has learned to paddle around all by itself on its hind legs, and says "poppa" and "momma." It is certainly a new species. This resemblance to words may be purely accidental, of course, and may have no purpose or meaning; but even in that case it is still extraordinary, and is a thing which no other bear can do. This imitation of speech, taken together with general absence of fur and entire absence of tail, sufficiently indicates that this is a new kind of bear. The further study of it will be exceedingly interesting. Meantime I will go off on a far expedition among the forests of the north and make an exhaustive search. There must certainly be another one somewhere, and this one will be less dangerous when it has company of its own species. I will go straightway; but I will muzzle this one first.

THREE MONTHS LATER.—It has been a weary, weary hunt, yet I have had no success. In the meantime, without stirring from the home-estate, she has caught another one! I never saw such luck. I might have hunted these woods a hundred years, I never would have run across that thing.

NEXT DAY.—I have been comparing the new one with the old one, and it is perfectly plain that they are the same breed. I was going to stuff one of them for my collection, but she is prejudiced against it for some reason or other; so I have relinquished the idea, though I think it is a mistake. It would be an irreparable loss to science if they should get away. The old one is tamer than it was, and can laugh and talk like the parrot, having learned this, no doubt, from being with the parrot so much, and having the imitative faculty in a highly developed degree. I shall be astonished if it turns out to be a new kind of parrot; and yet I ought not to be astonished, for it has already been everything else it could think of, since those first days when it was a fish. The new one is as ugly now as the old one was at first; has the same sulphur-and-raw-meat complexion and the same singular head without any fur on it. She calls it Abel.

TEN YEARS LATER.—They are boys; we found it out long ago. It was their coming in that small, immature shape that fooled us; we were not used to it. There are some girls now. Abel is a good boy, but if Cain had stayed a bear it would have improved him. After all these years, I see that I was mistaken about Eve in the beginning; it is better to live outside the Garden with her than inside it without her. At first I thought she talked too much; but now I should be sorry to have that voice fall silent and pass out of my life. Blessed be the chestnut that brought us near together and taught me to know the goodness of her heart and the sweetness of her spirit!

Famous Visitors at Niagara Falls.

By Thomas R. Slicer.

THE earliest description in literature of the Falls of Niagara was made by the Priest and Historian (?) Father Hennepin, the associate of the explorer La Salle, who built in 1679 the Griffin, to which appertains the honor of being the first vessel to sail the Great Lakes.

The reference is entitled " A description of the Fall of the River Niagara which is to be seen betwixt the Lake Ontario and that of Erie."

We give the commonly accepted version:

" Betwixt the Lake Ontario and Erie, there is a vast and prodigious Cadence of Water, which falls down after a surprising and astonishing manner, insomuch that the Universe does not afford its parallel. 'Tis true, Italy and Suedeland boast of some such things; but we may well say they are but sorry patterns, when compared to this of which we now speak. At the foot of this horrible Precipice, we meet with the River Niagara, which is not above a quarter of a league broad, but is wonderfully deep in some places. It is so rapid above this Descent, that it violently hurries down the wild beasts while endeavoring to pass it to feed on the other side, they not being able to withstand the force of its Current, which inevitably casts them headlong above Six Hundred feet high.[1]

"This wonderful Downfall is compounded of two cross-streams of Water, and two Falls, with an isle sloping along the middle of it. The waters which fall from this horrible Precipice, do foam and boyl after the most hideous manner imaginable; making an outrageous noise, more terrible than that of Thunder; for when the wind blows out of the South, their dismal roaring may be heard more than Fifteen Leagues off.[2]

"The River *Niagara* having thrown itself down this incredible Precipice, continues its impetuous course for Two Leagues together, to the great Rock above-mentioned, with inexpressible rapidity. But having passed that, its impetuosity relents, gliding along more gently for the other Two Leagues, till it arrives at the Lake Ontario or Frontenac.

"Any Bark or greater Vessel may pass from the Fort to the foot of this huge Rock above-mentioned. This Rock lies to the Westward, and is cut off from the Land by the River Niagara about Two Leagues further down than the great Fall, for which Two Leagues the people are obliged to transport their goods

---

1. ! ! ! This is too many "feet high." It was necessary, that it might be seen from the shores of France.

2. ! ! ! It was a long way to France and facts were made to correspond on account of the perspective.

overland; but the way is very good; and the Trees are very few, chiefly Firrs and Oakes.

"From the great Fall unto this Rock, which is to the West of the River, the two brinks of it are so prodigious high, that it would make one tremble to look steadily upon the water, rolling along with a rapidity not to be imagined· Were it not for this vast Cataract, which interrupts Navigation, they might sail with Barks or greater Vessels, more than Four Hundred and Fifty Leagues, crossing the Lake of Hurons, and reaching even to the farther end of the Lake of Illinis, which two Lakes we may easily say are little Seas of fresh Water."

There are other accounts by Tonti, Hontan and other early voyagers, but they are not especially to the purpose of this recital.

At the beginning of the present century, there limped, with an ankle sprained, to the shores of Lake Erie, from the borders of the forest a young Englishman, whose tastes and conceit were in strong contrast to the primitive simplicity of the scene on which he entered.

Perhaps no greater tribute has ever been paid to the charm of the Falls of Niagara than is suggested by the fact that they reconciled the mind of Tom Moore to the disgusting experiences of travel in America, where to his thinking the promiscuous hudling together of all sorts of people in the stagecoaches was a symbol of the mixed character of a Republican Government. A man who had been petted by an indulgent family and flattered by a social circle, which sang his songs and laughed at his wit, found the unsettled society of the New World not easy to adjust to his fastidious taste; he had done us the honor to look over our Country, and had done it up in his letters as " an interesting world, which with all the defects and disgusting peculiarities of its natives, gives every promise of no very distant competition with the first powers of the Eastern hemisphere."

When the Valleys of the Mohawk and the Genesee had been traversed, Moore was so much touched by their natural beauty that he exclaims: " Such scenery as there is around me! it is quite dreadful that any heart, born for sublimities, should be doomed to breathe away its hours amidst the miniature productions of this world, without seeing what shapes nature *can* assume, what wonders God *can* give birth to."

But he had not yet seen the Falls. He is about to start upon his journey to the Falls of Niagara in a wagon. On July 22d he sends back by the driver of the wagon a letter to be forwarded to his mother, written from upper Chippewa: " Just arrived within a mile and a half of the Falls of Niagara, and their tremendous roar at this moment sounding in my ears." Two days later he writes: " I have seen the Falls, and am all rapture and amazement. . . Arrived at Chippewa within three miles of the Falls to dinner Saturday, July 21st. That evening walked toward the Falls, but got no further than the Rapids, which gave us a prelibation of the grandure we had to expect.[1]

"Next day, Sunday, July 22d, went to visit the Falls.[2] Never shall I forget the impressions I felt at the first glimpse of them which we got as the carriage passed over the hill that overlooks them. We were not near enough to be agitated by the terrific effects of the scene; but saw through the trees this mighty flow of waters descending with calm magnificence, and received enough of its grandure to set imagination on the wing; imagination which even at Niagara can outrun reality.[3]

' I felt as if approaching the very residence of the Deity; the tears started into my eyes; and I remained for moments after we had lost sight of the scene, in that delicious absorption which pious enthusiasm alone can produce. We arrived at the New Ladder and de-

---

1. "Prelibations" are no longer to be had in the neighborhood of the Rapids; we mention this to save disappointment to any tourists who may inquire for them.

2. The Falls still fall on Sunday; no mention was included as to the Falls of Niagara in the petition to Congress respecting the Sunday-closing of the Exposition. The Falls ran nearly dry in 1848, but this was not due to any Act of Congress or to sympathy with the French Revolution, but was caused by an ice gorge at the outlet of Lake Erie.

3. This has not been the experience of the greater poets, Lowell, Longfellow and Bryant, none of whom have tried to describe the Falls in poetry; but the remark about imagination was made by Tom Moore in 1804, when imagination was stronger than it is now.

scended to the bottom. Here all its awful sublimities rushed full upon me. But the former exquisite sensation was gone. I now saw all. The string that had been touched by the first impulse, and which fancy would have kept forever in vibration, now rested at Reality. Yet though there was no more to imagine, there was much to feel. My whole heart and soul ascended toward the Divinity in a swell of devout admiration, which I never before experienced. . . . Oh! bring the Atheist here, and he cannot return an Atheist!"[1.]

The chief value of these attempts at description is not in that they do describe or fail to describe this natural phenomenon, but that they do describe the mind of the beholder; for it is ever a fact that when a great subject is dealt with by the human mind we get a double lesson; if the mind be competent we get a description of the subject, but in any event we get a portrait of the mind. In no instance does this more appear than in the contrasting way in which Niagara claimed the attention of three noted women: Mrs. Jameson, Harriet Martineau and Margaret Fuller. One would suppose that Mrs. Jameson's sense of beauty in

---

[1.] This is a miscalculation of human powers of resistance; Col. Robert Ingersoll has been to the Falls recently and expressed disapproval of them; he seemed to think that no really kind Being would turn loose such a quantity of water at once, and shock the human mind so rudely; he then turned his back on the Falls, and meditated on the anniversary of the birth of Lincoln, which he had spoken upon the day before. Those who accompanied the Colonel had some difficulty in fitting Abraham Lincoln into a World of Accidents. But they were only foolish people who believed in God.

Art would have prepared her mind for at least an ecstasy; or was it that her mind already winged for the flights of imagination, and used to dealing with art-forms in the galleries of Europe, did not find it easy to place itself *en rapport* with a canvas so large, as that on which the beauties of Niagara are painted by an unseen hand, in colors which are never two moments alike. Whatever may be the psychological reason, it is necessary to relate that Mrs. Jameson *would rather not have seen Niagara.* It was in 1837 that her visit was made to the Falls in the last part of January of that year. When she had stood face to face with them she exclaims: " Well, I have seen these cataracts of Niagara which have thundered in my mind's ear ever since I can remember—which have been my childhood's thought, my youth's desire, since first my imagination was awakened to wonder and to wish. I have beheld them; and shall I whisper it to you?—but, O tell it not among the Philistines!—I wish I had not! I wish they were still a thing to behold—a thing to be imagined, hoped, and anticipated—something to live for—the reality has displaced from my mind an illusion far more magnificent than itself.[1]—I have no words for my disappointment, yet I have not the presumption to suppose that all I have heard and read of Niagara is false or exaggerated[2]—

---

1. Later on we will see that in the estimation of magicians, like Hawthorne, it is advisable to go to the Falls after leaving our imaginations at home.
2. Nothing except the first measurements and the early geological guesses and most of the poetry and all of the pictures, except those in this volume.

that every expression of astonishment, enthusiasm, rapture, is affectation or hyperbole. No! it must be my own fault. Terni, and some of the Swiss cataracts leaping from their mountains, have affected me a thousand times more than all the immensity of Niagara. Oh, I could beat myself! and now there is no help!—the first moment, the first impression, is over—is lost; something is gone that cannot be restored. What has come over my soul and senses? I am no longer Anna—I am metamorphosed—I am translated—I am an ass's head, a clod, a wooden spoon, a fat weed growing on Lethe's bank, a stock, a stone, a petrifaction,—for have I not seen Niagara, the wonder of wonders; and felt—no words can tell *what* disappointment!"

The fact is, Mrs. Jameson had seen her Swiss cataracts to so little purpose that she seemed to be gazing into the sky for the beginning of the Falls of Niagara, and was surprised, when looking out from a high hill, to find that they were below her. She says: "My Imagination had been so impressed by the vast height of the Falls,[1] that I was constantly looking in an upward direction, when, as we came to the brow of the hill, my companion suddenly checked the horses, and exclaimed, 'The Falls!' I was not for an instant aware of their presence; we were yet at a distance looking *down* upon them; and I saw at one

---

1. Father Hennepin's "600 feet," probably.

glance a flat extensive plain; the sun having withdrawn its beams for a moment, there was neither light nor shade, nor colour. In the midst were seen the two great cataracts, but merely as a feature in the wide landscape.[1] The sound was by no means overpowering.[2] And the clouds of spray which Fannie Butler called so beautifully the "everlasting incense of the waters," now condensed, 'ere they rose, by the excessive cold, fell round the base of the cataracts in fleecy folds, just concealing that furious embrace of the waters above, and the waters below.[3] All the associations which in imagination I had gathered round the scene, its appalling terrors, its soul-subduing beauty, power, and height, and velocity, and immensity, were all diminished in effect, or wholly lost. I was quite silent—my soul sank within me." It would seem from the account of Mrs. Jameson that she had a most practical mind, for she was evidently delighted by the fact that a "little Yankee boy, with a shrewd sharp face, and twinkling black eyes, could not palm off a flock of gulls on her for eagles." The one sense of comfort that visited her arises from the fact that

1. That minimizing word "merely" has not often found place in the Niagara vocabulary.

2. "The roar of Niagara," as it is called, is the mellow chord of the full organ (see article in Scribner's Magazine by Eugene Thayer), and people who have expected to be deafened by a kind of Infinite Factory are surprised to find that they have no trouble in conversing together.

3. We shall see, however, later, that this which seemed an additional disappointment to Mrs. Jameson impressed Anthony Trollope as the most beautiful of all the Niagara phenomena.

though the Falls were not complementary to her mood, the smart boy was complimentary to her smartness, saying, "Well, now you be dreadful smart—smarter than many folks that come here." She tried the Falls from every point and found them from every point of view equally trying, and confesses at last, "The Falls did not make on my mind the impression that I had anticipated, perhaps for that reason, even because I had *anticipated* it; but ' it was sung to me in my cradle,' as the Germans say, that I should live to be disappointed—even in the Falls of Niagara."[1]

No two women could have been more unlike than Mrs. Jameson and Margaret Fuller, and yet one is haunted with the feeling that although Mrs. Jameson has so eloquently described "Art, sacred and legendary," Margaret Fuller was no less than Mrs. Jameson a soul sensitive to all influences in Art; but she lifts her eyes to the great Cataract and sees it by the light that fell from the mysterious and sacred center of her own impenetrable soul. She says[2] "The spectacle is, for once, great enough to fill the whole life, and supersede thought, giving us only its own presence. ' It is good to be here ' is the best as it is the simplest expression that occurs to the mind." Was

---

[1]. When foreigners cross the Atlantic they ought not to get the idea that Niagara is *the Atlantic set on edge;* and yet advice seems useless, for our aesthetic friend and epigramatic dramatist, Oscar Wilde, found the Atlantic disappointing. It is difficult to adjust the Atlantic and Niagara to certain types of mind. But as St. Paul remarks, "This is a great mystery."

[2]. At Home and Abroad, or Things and Thoughts in America and Europe.

it a lingering, half-conscious recollection that that phrase is a part of the story of The Transfiguration,[1] that she immediately adds: "We have been here eight days?" She says, further: "So great a sight soon satisfies, making us content with itself and with what is less than itself. Our desires once realized, haunt us again less readily. Having 'lived one day,' we would depart and become worthy to live another. My nerves too much braced up by such an atmosphere, do not well bear the continual stress of sight and sound. For here there is no escape from the weight of perpetual creation; all other forms and motions come and go, the tide rises and recedes, the wind, at its mightiest, moves in gales and gusts, but there is really an incessant, an indefatigable motion. Awake or asleep, there is no escape; still this rushing round you and through you. It is in this way I have most felt the grandeur—something eternal, if not infinite.

"At times a secondary music arises; the Cataract seems to seize its own rythm and sing it over again so that the ear and soul are roused by a double vibration. This is some effect of the wind, causing echoes to the thundering anthem. It is very sublime, giving the effect of a spiritual repetition through all the spheres."[2]

---

[1]. Luke, ix; 28.

[2]. This is that range of the full-organ again, to which Mr. Thayer's suggestive article upon the music of Niagara Falls refers.

Margaret Fuller speaks of Niagara as "the one object in the world that would not disappoint."[1]

She says of the Falls: "Daily their proportions widened and towered upon my sight, and I got, at last, a proper foreground for these sublime distances. Before coming away I think I really saw the full wonder of the scene. After a while it so drew me into itself as to inspire an undefined dread, such as I never knew before, such as may be felt when death is about to usher us into a new existence. The perpetual trampling of the waters seized my senses. I felt that no other sound, however near, could be heard, and would start and look behind me for a foe. I realized the identity of that mood of nature in which these waters were poured down with absorbing force, with that in which the Indian was shaped on the same soil."

There is a touch of nature in Margaret Fuller's confession, "The Whirlpool I like very much." She was quite capable of making her friends feel that she could be as "sternly solemn," as impenetrable to the eye, as the Whirlpool itself. The poetic side of her nature was satisfied with the beautiful forest on Goat Island and that wealth of wild flowers of which it was said by Sir Joseph Hooker, that more varieties were to be found on Goat Island than anywhere else in America in the same expanse of wild wood.

---

1. It was easier for people "to get on" with Mrs. Jameson; but there was something about Niagara that found in Margaret Fuller a congenial expansiveness; and perheps it required something like Niagara to make her properly expand.

Harriet Martineau's impressions were derived from a point not described by either of the other women before named. It was on her second visit to Niagara that we have from her a description of her sensations in passing *behind the American Fall*.

Miss Martineau says: " From the moment that I perceived that we were actually behind the Cataract, and not in a mere cloud of spray, the enjoyment was intense. I not only saw the watery curtain before me like the tempest-driven snow, but by momentary glances could see the crystal roof of one of the most wonderful of Nature's palaces. The precise point at which the flood quitted the rock was marked by a gush of silvery light, which of course was brighter where the waters were shooting forward, than below where they fell perpendicularly." She then describes quite graphically her successful effort to reach Termination Rock. It would be difficult to imagine Miss Martineau seeing the end of her journey, and *not reaching it*.

We turn now to another English mind, interested in an intense way in human welfare, interested as Miss Martineau was, but how different in the expression of that interest! It is a strange contrast which it exhibits in presence of the great flood.

The mind that created Mr. Pickwick and David Copperfield will have something to say original even about Niagara. But Dickens was at heart a poet. His Fiction was perhaps exaggeration of the facts, but the facts were forever fixed by it; and brought face to face with Nature in such aspects as make the mighty Cataract we should expect to have called out from his soul that religious response which mystery and majesty never failed to evoke; and we are not disappointed. He says: " Whenever the train halted I listened for the roar, and was constantly straining my eyes in the direction where I knew the Falls must be, from seeing the river rolling on toward them; every moment expecting to behold the spray. Within a few minutes of our stopping, not before, I saw two great white clouds rising up slowly and majestically from the depths of the earth. That was all. At length we alighted and then for the first time I heard the mighty rush of water, and felt the ground tremble under my feet." He climbed down the steep and slippery bank, made insecure to the foot by rain and half-melted ice, to face the Fall, but was not content with this view. A little ferry-boat that then plied from one side to the other carried him and his party across the river below the Fall, while he was more and more astounded by the vastness of the scene. He says: " It was not until I came on Table Rock, and looked, Great Heaven! on what a fall of bright green water—that it came upon me in its full majesty. Then when I felt how near to my Creator I was standing, the first effect, and the enduring one, instant and lasting, of the tremendous spectacle, was peace. Peace of mind, tranquility, calm recollections of the dead, great thoughts of eternal rest and happiness; nothing of gloom or terror. Niagara was at once stamped upon my heart, an image of beauty, to remain there, changeless and indelible, until its pulses cease to beat, forever. I never stirred in all that time from the Canadian side whither I had gone at first. I never crossed the river again; for I knew there were people on the other shore, and in such a place it is natural to shun strange company.[1] To wander to and fro all day and see the Cataracts from all points of view; to stand upon the edge of the Great Horse Shoe Fall, marking the hurried water gathering strength as it approached the verge, yet seeming, too, to pause before it shot into the gulf below; to gaze from the river's level up at the torrent as it came streaming down; to climb the neighboring heights and watch it through the trees, and see the wreathing water in the rapids, hurrying on to take its fearful plunge; to linger in the shadow of the solemn rocks three miles below, watching the river as, stirred by no visible cause, it heaved and eddied and awoke the echoes, being troubled yet far down beneath the surface, by its giant leap; to have Niagara before me, lighted by the sun and the moon, red in the day's decline, and grey as evening slowly fell upon it; to look upon it every day, and wake up in the night and hear its ceaseless voice,

---

1. The contrast in this particular between Dickens and N. P. Willis opens up an interesting chapter in the natural differences in literary temperament, as it deals with human life.

this was enough. I think, in every quiet season now, still do those waters roll and leap and roar and tumble, all day long; still are the rainbows spanning them a hundred feet below. Still when the sun is on them do they shine and glow like molten gold. Still when the day is gloomy, do they fall like snow, or seem to crumble away like the front of a great chalk cliff, or roll down the rock like dense white smoke. But always does this mighty stream appear to die as it comes down, and always from its unfathomable grave arises that tremendous ghost of spray and mist, which is never laid; which has haunted this place with the same dread solemnity since darkness brooded on the Deep, and that first flood before the Deluge—Light—came rushing on Creation at the word of God."

Nothing could be more characteristic of that strange commingling of wonder and reserve in a human nature than the way in which Hawthorne came toward, and yet not quite *to* the Falls again and again. He says: "I had lingered away from it and wandered to other scenes. My treasury of anticipated enjoyments comprising all the wonders of the world had nothing else so magnificent; I was loathe to exchange the pleasures of hope for those of memory so soon." There was nothing of the severe Yankee temperament in Hawthorne's attitude toward this great scene; it was rather that infusion of French self-indulgence which made him dread to count a delight, as a thing he *had had*. He says: "At length the day came, I walked toward Goat Island and crossed the bridge; above and below me were the rapids, a river of impetuous snow, with here and there a dark rock amid its whiteness, resisting all the physical fury as any cold spirit did the moral influences of the scene."

We may go with Hawthorne along the path if we will. "On reaching Goat Island, which separates the two great segments of the Falls, I chose the right hand path and followed it to the edge of the American Cascade; there, while the falling sheet was yet invisible, I saw the vapor that never vanishes and the eternal rainbow of Niagara. I gained an insulated rock and observed a broad sheet of brilliant and unbroken foam, not shooting in a curved line from the top of the precipice, but falling headlong down from height to depth." When Hawthorne had made the round of the Island and had seen the Falls from every available *coin of vantage*, he stops, as was his custom, to take an account of his mental sensations. "Were my long desires fulfilled, and have I seen Niagara? But would I had never heard of Niagara until I beheld it! Blessed were the wanderers of old, who heard its deep roar sounding through the woods, as a summons to its unknown wonder, and approached its awful brink in all the freshness of native feeling; had its own mysterious voice been the first to warn me of its existence, then indeed, I might have fallen down and worshipped; but

I had come haunted with a vision of foam and fury and dizzy cliffs, and an ocean tumbling down out of the sky—a scene, in short, which nature had too much good taste and calm simplicity to realize. My mind had struggled to adapt these false aspects to the reality, and finding the effort vain, a wretched sense of disappointment weighed me down. I climbed the precipice and threw myself on the earth feeling that I was unworthy to look at the great Falls and careless about observing them again." It would be strange, indeed, if the author of "Twice-Told-Tales" did not find some "wonder" in this repetition to him in other terms of that which he had already imagined. So he says of the night, which succeeded this first day-visit: "As there has been, and may be for ages to come, a rushing sound was heard, as if a great tempest was sweeping through the air. It mingled in my dreams and made them full of storm and whirlwind. Whenever I awoke I heard this dread sound in the air, and the windows rattling as with a mighty blast. I could not rest again until, looking forth, I saw how bright the stars were and that every leaf in the garden was motionless. *Never was summer night more calm to the eye, nor a gale of autumn louder to the ear.* The rushing sound proceeds from the Rapids and the rattling of the casements is but an effect of the vibration of the whole house shaken by the jar of the Cataract. The noise of the Rapids draws the attention from the true voice of Niagara, which is a dull muffled thunder, resounding between the cliffs. I spent a wakeful hour at midnight in distinguishing between its reverberations, and rejoiced to find that my former awe and enthusiasm were reviving.

" Gradually and after much contemplation, I came to know by my own feelings that Niagara is indeed a wonder of the world; and not the less wonderful because time and thought must be employed in comprehending it." And here follows the sanest advice to those who have felt at first the sense of disappointment that the cataract is not so great as they had conceived : " Casting aside all preconceived notions and preparation to be awe-struck or delighted, the beholder must stand beside it in the simplicity of his heart, suffering the mighty scene to work its own impression. Night after night I dreamed of it, and was gladdened every morning by the sensations of growing capacity to enjoy it."

This description by Hawthorne, from which these brief quotations have been made, contains nothing truer to a fine nature than that in which he states his last impressions of the Falls: " I sat upon Table Rock; never before had my mind been in such perfect unison with the scene. There were intervals when I was conscious of nothing but the great river rolling calmly into the abyss ; rather descending than precipitating itself, and acquiring ten-fold majesty from its unhurried

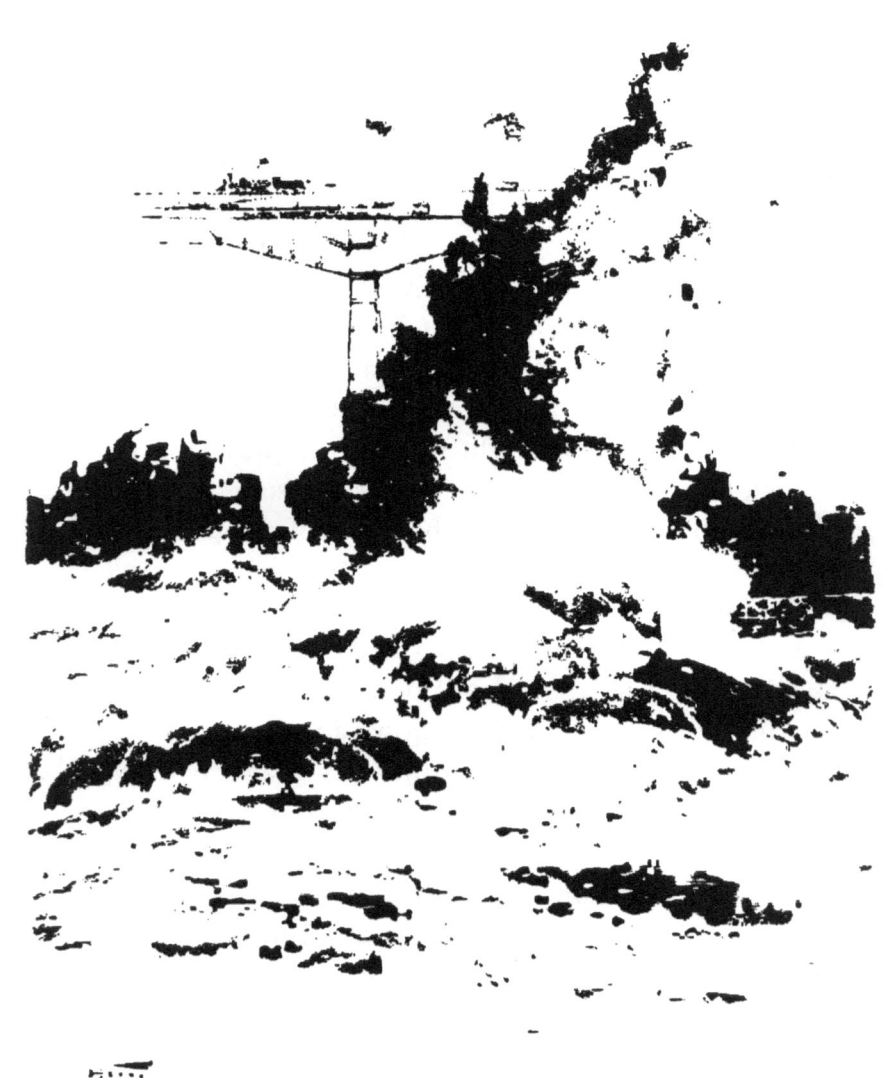

motion. It came like the march of destiny; it was not taken by surprise, but seemed to have anticipated in all its course through the broad lakes that it must pour their collected waters down this height." The impression made by the water where it falls is noted by Hawthorne and by few besides—the stillness with which it slips away from the stroke of the cataract, seeming scarcely to move in its eddies, which are only the slight surface-struggle of the great depth of waters in the narrow gorge into which it falls. He says of this: " When the observer has stood still and perceived no lull in the storm and stress, that the vapor and the foam are as everlasting as the rock which produces them, all this turmoil assumes a sort of calmness; it soothes while it awes the mind."

Hawthorne is quite right in feeling that Niagara cannot be seen " in company " or worshipped by platoons; for one wants to steal to some unobserved retreat from which to look out and feel, as he says, " The enjoyment which becomes rapture, more rapturous because no poet shared it, nor wretch devoid of poetry profaned it; the spot so famous through the world was all mine." This same feeling was shared by Charles Kingsley. He says: " I long to simply look on in silence whole days at the exquisite beauty of form and color."

To Dean Stanley the first sight of the Falls seemed " an epoch, like the first view of the pyramids, or the snow-clad range of the Alps." His first view of it was at midnight under a full moon. To him it seemed an " emblem of the devouring activity and ceaseless, restless, beating whirlpool of existence in the United States. But into the moonlight sky there rose a cloud of spray twice as high as the Falls themselves, silent, majestic, immovable. In that silver column, glittering in the moonlight, I saw an image of the future of American destiny, of the pillar of light which should emerge from the distractions of the present—a likeness of the buoyancy and hopefulness which characterises you, both as individuals and as a nation."

Professor Tyndall's mind has not been robbed of its sentiment by the minute contemplation of incident and detail, as Darwin suffered an *atrophy* in the appreciation of poetry as he himself confesses. It is to Professor Tyndall we owe this bit of poetic prose in which he describes the Whirlpool : " The scene presented itself as one of holy seclusion and beauty. I went down to the water's edge where the weird loneliness and loveliness seems to increase. The basin is enclosed by high and almost precipitous banks, covered, when I was there, with russet woods. A kind of mystery attaches to gyrating water, due perhaps to the fact that we are to some extent ignorant of the direction of its force. It is said that at a certain point in the whirlpool pine trees are sucked down to be ejected mysteriously elsewhere. The water is the brightest emerald green; the gorge through which it escapes is narrow and the motion of the river swift though silent; the surface is steeply inclined but it is perfectly unbroken. There are no lateral waves, no ripples, with their breaking bubbles to raise a murmur, while the depth is here too great to allow the inequality of the bed to ruffle the surface. Nothing can be more beautiful than this sloping, liquid mirror formed by the Niagara in sliding from the Whirlpool."

If one wishes to know the measure of the mind of N. P. Willis, he may gain it from Willis's description of the Falls of Niagara. It does not suit our purpose to quote it here. It is the same mixture of poetry and commonplace, of incident and contact with people, that made Mr. Willis the ideal magazine writer of that time.

It is strange to note how different points seem to be the center of focussed thought to different minds. To Mrs. Trollope it was the centre of the Horse-shoe, which seemed "the most utterly inconceivable." "The famous torrent converges there, as the heavy mass pours in, twisted, rolled and curled together; it gives the idea of irresistible power such as no other object ever conveyed to me. The mighty caldron into which the deluge pours, the hundred silvery torrents congregated around its verge, the smooth and solemn movement with which it rolls its massive volume over the rock, the liquid emerald of its long unbroken waters, the fantastic wreaths which spring to meet it, and then the shadowy mist that veils the horrors of the crash below, constitute a scene almost too enormous in its features for man to look upon."

To Charles Dudley Warner it is at a different point the mind pauses and feels its most impressive moment. " Nowhere is the river so terrible as where it rushes, as if maddened by its narrow bondage through the cañon ; flowing down the precipice and forced into this contracting space, it fumes and tosses and raves with a vindictive fury, driving on in a passion that has almost a human quality in it ; and restrained by the walls of stone from being destructive, it seems to rave at its own impotence, and when it reaches the Whirlpool it is like a hungry animal, returning and licking the shore for the prey it has missed."

Professor Richard Proctor is impressed by the terrible force of the Niagara at the same spot. Speaking of the fatal attempt of Captain Webb to swim the Whirlpool Rapids he says : " He maybe did not know what a rough estimate of the enierges at work in Niagara should have shown, that amid that mass of water which descends from the basin below the Falls to the engulfing vortex of the Whirlpool, the body of the biggest and strongest living creature must be as powerless as a drop of water in mid-Atlantic."

When Anthony Trollope assures us in his discussions upon novel-writing that all that a novelist needs is a table and chair with a bit of shoemaker's wax upon the seat of it, we suspect that he is only excusing his own voluminous production. He does not lack poetic inspiration as the following quotations will show: "But we will go on at once to the glory and thunder and the majesty, and the wrath of that upper hell of waters. We are still on Goat Island. Advancing beyond the path leading down to the lower Fall, we come to that point of the Island at which the waters of the main river begin to descend. Go down to the end of the wooden bridge, seat yourself on the rail, and then sit 'till all the outer world is lost to you. There is no grander spot about Niagara than this. The waters are absolutely around you. Here, seated on the rail of the bridge, you will not see the whole depth of the Fall. In looking at the grandest works of nature and of art too, I fancy it is never well to see all. There should be something left to the imagination, and much should be half concealed in mystery. The greatest charm of a mountain range is that wild feeling, there must be something strange, unknown, desolate in those far-off valleys beyond. And so here, at Niagara, that converging rush of waters may fall down, down at once into a hell of rivers, for what the eye can see. It is glorious to watch them in their first curve over the rocks. They come green as a bank of emeralds; but with a fitful flying color, as though conscious that in one moment more they would be dashed into spray and rise into air pale as driven snow. The vapor rises high into the air and is gathered there, visible always as a permanent white cloud over the cataract; but the bulk of the spray which fills the lower hollow of that horseshoe is like a tumult of snow.

"This you will not fully see from your seat on the rail. The head of it rises ever and anon out of that caldron below, but the caldron itself will be invisible. It is ever so far down, far as your own imagination can sink it. But your eyes will rest full upon the curve of the waters. The shape you will be looking at is that of a horseshoe, but of a horseshoe miraculously deep from toe to heel; and this depth becomes greater as you sit there. That which at first was only great and beautiful, becomes gigantic and sublime till the mind is at a loss to find an epithet for its own use. To realize Niagara you must sit there 'till you see nothing else than that which you have come to see. You will hear nothing else and think of nothing else. At length you will be at one with the tumbling river before you. You will find yourself among the waters as though you belonged to them. The cool liquid green will run through your veins, and the voice of the cataract will be the expression of your heart. You will fall, as the bright waters fall, rushing down into your new world with no hesitation and with no dismay; and you will rise again as the spray rises, bright, beautiful and pure.

"One of the great charms of Niagara consists in this —that over and above that one great object of wonder and beauty; there is so much little loveliness; loveliness especially of water, I mean. There are little rivulets running here and there over little falls, with pendent boughs above them, and stones shining under their shallow depths. As the visitor stands and looks through the trees, the Rapids glitter before him, and then hide themselves behind islands. They glitter and sparkle in far distances under the bright foliage till the remembrance is lost and one knows not which way they run.

"Of all the sights in this earth of ours which tourists travel to see—at least of all those which I have seen—I am inclined to give the palm to Niagara. I know no other one thing so beautiful, so glorious, so powerful."

When we know that Bayard Taylor visited the Falls of Niagara we instantly desire to know what impression was made upon a mind which had contemplated such a wide range and variety as this great traveler had seen and had elsewhere described. He thus brings his poetic imagination to the contemplation: "The picturesque shores of the river, the splendid green of the water, and the lofty line of the upper plateau in front, crowned with Brock's monument, and divided by the dark yawning gorge of Niagara, form a fitting vestibule to the grand *adytum* beyond. The chasm grows wider, deeper and more precipitous with every mile, until having seen the Suspension Bridge apparently floating in mid-air on your right, you look ahead, and two miles off you catch a glimpse of the emerald crest of Niagara, standing fast and fixed above its shifting chaos of snowy spray.

"I have seen the Falls in all weathers and at all seasons, but to my mind the winter view is most beautiful. I saw them first in the hard winter of 1854, when a hundred cataracts of ice hung from the cliffs on either side, when the masses of ice brought down from Lake Erie were wedged together at the foot, uniting the shores with a rugged bridge, and when every twig and every tree and bush in Goat Island was overlaid an inch deep with a coating of solid crystal. The air was still and the sun shone in a cloudless sky. The green of the Fall set in a landscape of sparkling silver, was infinitely more brilliant than in the summer, when it is balanced by the trees, and the rainbows were almost too glorious for the eye to bear. I was not impressed by the sublimity of the scene nor even by its terror, but solely by the fascination of its wonderful beauty, a fascination which constantly tempted me to plunge into that sea of fused emerald and lose myself in the dance of the rainbows. With each succeeding visit Niagara has grown in height, in power, in majesty, in solemnity; but I have seen its climax of beauty."

Reference has been made in this writing to the remarkable fact that the greater American poets have not attempted to describe Niagara. The fact is easily discernible in their writings; but the cause of this apparent neglect of a theme, which has tempted so many smaller singers must be sought in the laws of the human mind as affected by the contact of that which transcends all rhythmic expression. It would seem that the greater the gift of expression for the less overpowering appeal of Nature to the soul, the more impotent in *this presence* the poets have felt. There are not wanting indeed poems about Niagara, one which flows like the river itself, undamed for forty thousand lines; and in some of these individual lines there are perhaps several lines together which seem to catch the swing of the great Cataract; though at best they are a shrill piping to its mighty *diapason*; they are like the song of the wren on its bank. Even Mrs. Sigourney's lines are felt by her to be inadequate:

      Ah, who can dare
To lift the insect-trump of earthly hope,
Or love, or sorrow, 'mid the peal sublime
Of thy tremendous hymn? Even Ocean shrinks
Back from thy brotherhood and all his waves
Retire abashed. For he doth sometimes seem
To sleep like a spent laborer and recall
His wearied billows from their vexing play,
And lull them to a cradle calm; but thou
With everlasting, undecaying tide,
Dost rest not, night or day."
     *   *   *

      " Thou dost make the soul
A wondering witness of thy majesty,

> And as it presses with delirious joy
> To pierce thy vestibule, dost chain its step,
> And tame its rapture with a humbling view
> Of its own nothingness, bidding it stand
> In the dread presence of the Invisible,
> As if to answer to its God through thee."

These are perhaps the best of the lines written by Mrs. Sigourney; but their inadequacy is felt by any one who compares them with a moment's recollection of his own feelings in the presence they attempt to describe.

The lines of Lord Morpeth are well known, they seem most memorable for the sincere expression of that good will which he hoped might ever subsist between the nations, his own and America:

> " Oh! may thy waves which madden in thy deep
> *There* spend their rage nor climb the encircling steep;
> And till the conflict of thy surges cease
> The nations on thy banks repose in peace."

There seems to be a wide-spread conviction that the oft-quoted lines of John G. C. Brainard are " the noblest lines inspired by the great Cataract." They are notable as rising in the mind of a New England editor who had never seen the Falls, and are said to have been the work of a few moments—an improvisation:

"The thoughts are strange that crowd into my
    brain
While I look upward to thee. It would seem
As if God poured thee from ' His hollow hand '
And hung His bow upon thine awful front,
And spoke in that loud voice which seemed to
    him
Who dwelt in Patmos for his Savior's sake
' The sound of many waters,' and had bade
Thy flood to chronicle the ages back,
And notch His cent'ries in the eternal rock.

" Deep calleth unto Deep. And what are we
That hear the question of that voice sublime?
Oh! What are all the notes that ever rung
From war's vain trumpet by thy thundering side!
Yea, what is all the riot man can make
In his short life to thy unceasing roar!
And yet bold babbler, what art thou to Him
Who drowned a world and heaped the waters far
Above its loftiest mountains?—a light wave
That breaks and whispers of its Maker's might."

There are many other expressions of those who from all parts of the world have matched the feebleness of speech against the stress of feeling; but we forbear to quote further. The extracts given above will prove sufficient for their purpose if they constitute a pleasure to the receptive mind, susceptible to the influences of the scene they visit, and if they prove a gentle warning to the too eager expression of words which so often hide rather than reveal thought.

A : HISTORY : OF NIAGARA : FALLS
BY PETER : A : PORTER.

FAMOUS all over the world as Niagara is today, in its scenic, botanic, geologic and hydraulic aspects, it is equally famous, equally interesting, and equally instructive in its various and numerous historic features. And in using the words of our title we use them in their broadest and noblest sense, employing the word "historic" to cover all those multitudinous phases of this region's existence and condition at which a true student of history instinctively looks; we use the word Niagara, not in that circumscribed meaning which takes in only the Falls and their immediate surroundings, but make it cover both banks of this famous river from its source to its mouth. To treat of such a broad subject within the narrow limits of a few pages will permit of only the briefest reference to any point.

EARLY MENTIONS OF NIAGARA.

Just when white men first saw the Falls we cannot accurately say. This great Cataract was known in a general way to the Indians of North America, who dwelt far from it and who had never seen it, probably before Columbus sailed on his first voyage of discovery. At any rate, within fifty years after Columbus landed at San Salvador (to be exact, in 1535), its existence was well known to the Indians on the Gulf of the St. Lawrence, and, through them, to at least one boat-load of adventurous Europeans. In that year Jacques Cartier made his second voyage to this Continent, and the Indians told him in reply to his inquiries regarding the source of the St. Lawrence, that "after ascending many leagues among rapids and waterfalls he would reach a lake (Ontario), 140 or 150 leagues broad, at the western end of which the waters were wholesome and the winters mild; that a river emptied into it from the south which had its source in the country of the Iroquois; that beyond the lake he would find a cataract and a portage; then another lake (Erie) about equal to the former, which they had never explored." This is related by Marc Lescarbot, who in 1609 published his History of New France, in which he describes Cartier's second voyage. During the hundred years succeeding that voyage, the Falls may have been visited at any time, by any of the adventurous explorers, traders and seamen sent out by France to resume explorations in the New World, although they have left us no record of any such visitations. Samuel De Champlain in his "Des Sauvages," published in 1603 and describing his first voyage to the St. Lawrence in that year, refers to the

Falls in unmistakable language though not by name, and it is not probable that he ever saw them. In his 1613 volume, describing his voyages up to that date, he locates them very accurately on his map as a "waterfall," but not by name; and in his 1632 edition, he both locates them correctly, though not by their name, on his map and further refers to them in his description of the map itself. In 1641, the Jesuit Father L'Allement in his letters to his superior, speaking of the Indian tribes, refers to the " Neuter nation (Onguaarha), having the same name as the river;" and in 1648 the Jesuit Father Ragueneau in a similar letter says, " North of the Eries is a great lake fully 200 leagues in circumference called Erie, formed by the discharge of the *Mer Douce* (Lake Huron), which falls into a third lake called Ontario, though we call it Lake St. Louis, over a cataract of fearful height." In 1656 Sanson located the Falls accurately on his map and called them "Ongiara," and in 1660 De Creuxius in his *Historiae Canadensis* noted them as " Ongiara Catarractes." In 1678, Father Louis Hennepin, who accompanied La Salle, tells us that "he personally" visited the Falls, and in his first book, Louisiana, published in 1683, describing La Salle's explorations and adventures in this section of the country, applies the name Niagara both to the river and to the Falls, and gives the earliest, though a very brief description of the Falls themselves. In 1688, Coronellis's map of this region locates the Falls and first uses the name " Niagara " in cartography, a name used from that date without change. In 1691, Father Le Clercq in his " Establishment of the Faith " (from which work Father Hennepin is accused of plagiarizing certain parts of his famous "New Discovery"), also speaks of " Niagara Falls," but it is in Father Hennepin's " New Discovery " just referred to, published in 1697, that we find the first real description of them preserved to us in type, and in that volume is also given the first illustration of the Falls, which is reproduced in this work. A part of Hennepin's description is also quoted in another article in this book.

During the next fifty years Hennepin's works appeared in some forty-five editions and reproductions, and were translated into all the languages of Europe; and by these means and from descriptions of other travelers (notably that of Campanius Holm, in his New Sweden, published in 1702, and Baron La Hontan's voyages published in 1703), Niagara became generally known to Europeans. It was reserved for Charlevoix in 1721 accurately to reckon the height of the Falls and to correct other erroneous reports and descriptions of them published theretofore. We have thus briefly traced the history of the earliest knowledge and of the earliest literature of Niagara down to a comparatively recent date. From that time the bibliography of Niagara, including its cartography and illustrations of every kind, is so voluminous as to form in itself a distinct branch of our title on which for lack of space we cannot even touch.

THE NAME NIAGARA.

The Indian custom of giving their tribal name to, or taking it from, the chief natural feature of the country they inhabited (as proved by the nomenclature of the central and eastern states, as well as in the extensive literature on Indian subjects) tells us that a nation of this name inhabited the territory along the Niagara River on both sides ; but as there are forty different known ways of spelling the name, its orthography differs materially with various early authors.* This much, however, we know,—that when Hennepin first saw the Falls, *Niagara* was the local Indian spelling of the name ; "Niagara," the world accepted it ; and "Niagara" it has been ever since. According to the most general acceptance the name is derived from what is commonly known as the Iroquois language, and signifies " the thunder of the waters," though this appropriate and poetic significance has been questioned, and it is claimed by some that it signifies " neck," symbolizing the fact of the Niagara River being the connecting link between the two great lakes.

---

*A list of these are given in the Index volume of the Documentary History of the State of New York. The most commonly met with of these variations are Onguaarha, Ongiara, Onyakara, Iagara, Nicariaga, Ungiara, and Jagara.

The Neuter or Niagara nation of Indians (subsequently merged into the Iroquois) by whom the name was first adopted, would seem to have pronounced it Nyáh-ga-ráh, their language having no labial sounds, and all their words being spoken without closing the lips. The pronunciation Neé-ah-gara, sometimes heard nowadays, was probably also in common use later on; while in more modern Indian dialect, the sounding of every vowel being still continued, Ni-ah-gáh-rah, (accent on the third syllable), was the accepted, as it is the correct, pronunciation—the present pronunciation, without any pronounced accent on any syllable, being an adaptation of more recent years.

MODERN HISTORY.

The commencement of what may be termed the modern history of this region, dates back to that day in December, 1678, when, starting from the mouth of the Niagara River

> "A chieftain of the Iroquois, clad in a bison skin,
> Had let two travelers through the woods—
> La Salle and Hennepin."

to view the great cataract of which they had heard so much from their Indian allies on the St. Lawrence. As these three men stood there, they typified the nations—the French and the Indian—that for almost a hundred years were to control the destinies of this region; and in their personalities, " the chief, the soldier of the sword and the soldier of the cross," they exemplified the professions by means of which its conquest and civilization were to be effected.

In the two hundred years that have elapsed since that day, the Indian and the Frenchman have disappeared from this region; another and a stronger race has acquired possession of this territory, to be in turn dispossessed of half of it by her own descendants. And during those two hundred years, on the pages of their history and in the literature of France, England, Canada and the United States, the name *Niagara* is indelibly stamped as a prominent and integral part.

OWNERSHIP.

So far as the contention for, and the possession of, this famous region by the nations of the earth are concerned, we may divide its history into these main periods.

French claims on a broad basis by reason of early explorations and discoveries in the east, up to her real occupation by La Salle in 1678.

French occupation and sovereignty from that date, gradually, but regularly, and at last successfully disputed by the English in 1759.

English occupation and control from then till 1776.

English occupation till 1783, and from then of all land lying west of the Niagara River.

United States ownership and control of that part

lying east of the Niagara River from that date, although so far as Fort Niagara is concerned, England did not relinquish it till 1796.

FRENCH OCCUPATION.

The French, having early claimed all the Northeastern part of this continent from Labrador southwards as above noted, began at an early date to push their explorations and conquests westwards at first mainly along the line of the St. Lawrence River. Champlain, between 1603 and 1630, had done much to make France a paramount force in this section and to attach many of the Indians to her allegiance by siding with them in their tribal wars against their neighbors,— an alliance which in after years arrayed many Indian tribes against her and hastened her defeat.

On Dec. 6, 1878, La Salle, who, through love of his country and expectations of personal wealth, had labored long to extend the sovereignty of France, in a brig of ten tons and with a crew of sixteen persons entered the mouth of the Niagara River. He was on his westward journey, his objects being to make good by conquest the powers conferred upon him by the French king, to obtain for himself a monopoly of the fur trade, and to reach and control the mines of St. Barbe, in Louisiana; and as he went he intended to establish a chain of fortifications which both in war and the fur trade should be points of vantage for future generations.

True soldier that he was, he at once saw immense

strategic advantage of the point where Fort Niagara now stands, and to this day the correctness of his judgment has not been questioned. Here he built a trading post, and pursuing his way up the Niagara River to where Lewiston now stands, he built a fort of palisades; and carrying the anchors, cordage, etc., which he had brought for that purpose, up the so-called "Three Mountains" at Lewiston, he found a spot at the mouth of Cayuga Creek, about five miles above the Falls (where is to-day a hamlet bearing his name) where he built and launched the Griffon the first vessel that ever sailed the upper lakes. For almost a hundred years after this the history of the Niagara Frontier belongs to the French, though their sovereignty was attacked and at last overthrown by the English.

In 1687, Marquis De Nonville, returning from his expedition against the hostile Senecas, fortified La Salle's trading post at Fort Niagara. The following year it was abandoned and destroyed, but it was too valuable a point of vantage to be lost, and in 1725 it was rebuilt in stone by consent of the Iroquois.

The site of the present village of Lewiston, the head of navigation on the lower Niagara, was the commencement of a portage by which goods, ammunition, etc., were conveyed to a point about a mile and a half above the Falls, over a line which is still called the Portage Road; and for the purposes of this portage, from the edge of the river at the lower end of the rapids up the

"Three Mountains," was built a rude tramway on which, by means of ropes and windlasses, a car was raised and lowered. At what date this was first operated, we cannot tell, but it is claimed to have been the first of its kind in use in this country. Though noted on many maps no trace even of its foundations now remains. The Indians, naturally averse to manual labor, operated the tramway, taking their pay in rum and tobacco, otherwise unobtainable by them. The upper end of this portage was originally only a landing place for boats, but was gradually fortified until in 1750 it became a strong fort—called Fort Du Portage, or by some, Fort Little Niagara—to defend the French barracks and store houses which had been erected there. The Fort was burned in 1759 by Joncaire, who was in command when the British commenced their memorable campaign of that year, and Joncaire retreated to a station on Chippewa Creek. In that campaign General Prideaux, commanding the British forces in this section, and carrying out that portion of the general plan assigned to him, massed his forces on the shore of Lake Ontario, east of Fort Niagara, and demanded its surrender; this being refused, he laid siege to it. During the siege Prideaux was killed, and Sir William Johnson succeeded him and captured Fort Niagara, the last stronghold then held by the French in that long chain of forts connecting Canada with Louisiana. During the siege the French had sent re-inforcements from

Venango in Pennsylvania to the garrison of Niagara. They got as far as Navy Island (named Isle de Marine by the French), on which they had landed when they learned of the surrender of the Fort. On this island the French had recently built some small vessels, and to prevent these, as well as the two ships which brought down the re-inforcements from Venango, from falling into the hands of the victorious English, they took them over to Grand Island, at the northern end of which is a bay where they set them on fire, destroying them and sinking the useless hulls, from which circumstance the place is called Burnt Ship Bay to this day.

The British successes of 1759 made them masters of all this frontier and by 1761, Captain Joseph Schlosser of the British Army built a fort a little to the east of Fort Du Portage and named it after himself. Just below the site of that fort still stands a solitary stone chimney, the only relic left of all these fortifications. It was part of the old French barracks, alluded to above, at Fort Du Portage.

DEVIL'S HOLE MASSACRE.

The Indian nature is heartless and unforgiving. When Champlain in his trip to the lake which bears his name asked the assistance of the Senecas, he took their part in their tribal war against the Iroquois. Thus was laid the commencement of that partisanship of the various Indian tribes, some to the French and some to the English, which lasted throughout the

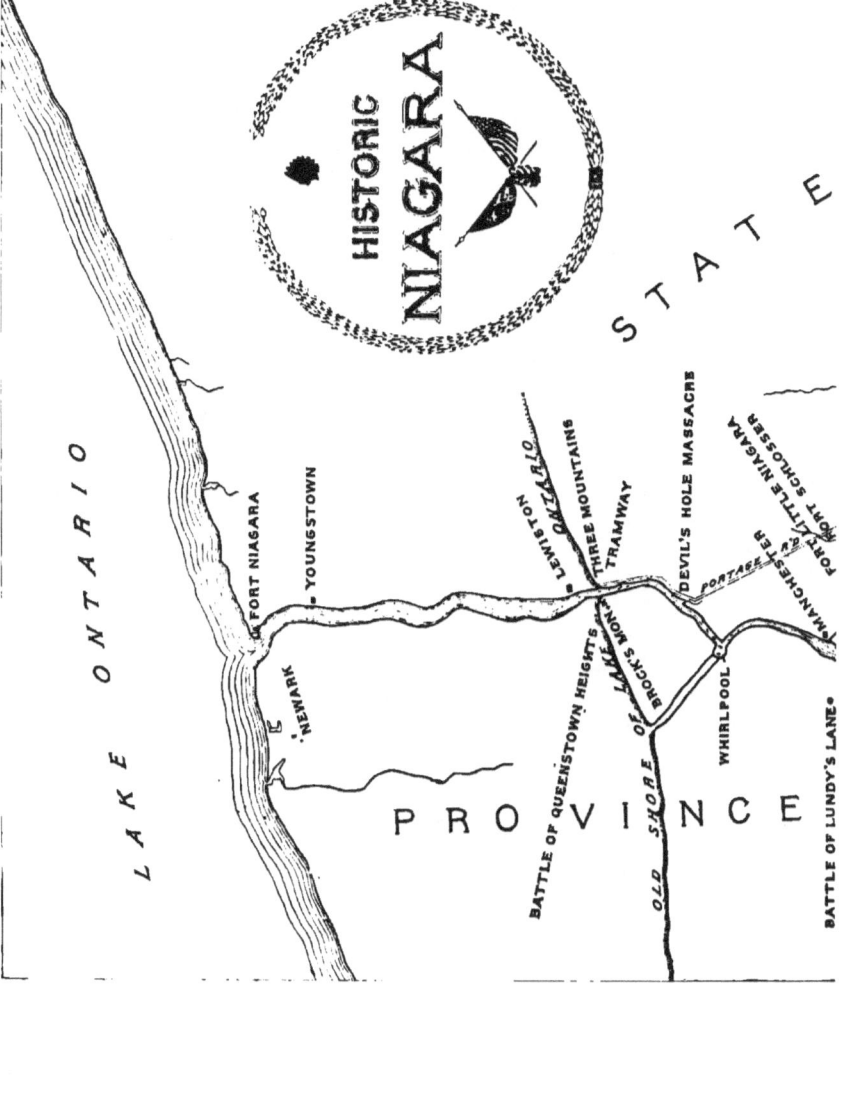

better part of the eighteenth century, and one of the results of which was that fatal tragedy on this frontier known as "The Devil's Hole Massacre."

After the British success of 1759 and their subsequent control of this territory, the Senecas, actuated by their inherited hatred of the English and incited probably by the French, commenced a bloody supplemental campaign in 1763. Knowing that the English were daily sending slightly guarded trains from Fort Niagara through Lewiston, where they had an auxiliary encampment, to Fort Schlosser, they planned an ambuscade and executed it with precision and fatal results. At the narrow pass at the Devil's Hole they ambushed the supply train, destroying it and killing all but three of the escort and drivers. They then ambushed the relieving force, which on hearing the firing had hastened from Lewiston, killing all but eight. It was a masterly example of Indian warfare executed with Indian cunning and Indian bloodthirstiness.

CESSIONS AND TREATIES.

By the treaty of 1763 France ceded to England all this region and all her Canadian possessions for which her armies and her missionaries had spent, during one hundred years, so much energy, so vast an amount of money, and so many lives.

In the spring of 1764 Sir William Johnson, supplementing the treaty of the preceding year, assembled all the Indians of this region, over 2,000 in number, including the hostile Senecas, at Fort Niagara, and acquired from them, for the English crown, the title to a large tract of land, including a strip eight miles in width, four miles wide on each side of the Niagara river for its entire length. At the same time the Senecas ceded to Sir William Johnson all the islands in the Niagara river. He in turn ceded them to the British Sovereign. So that at this time Niagara Falls, the grandest and most noted Cataract on the globe, was the *Koh-i-noor* of the English crown in the New World. Twelve years afterwards the Declaration of Independence was signed and the long revolutionary struggle for independence commenced. Had General Sullivan's campaign of 1779, as planned, been successful, he would have attacked Fort Niagara ; but disaster overtook him and the tide of revolution never reached the Niagara river in actual hostilities. In 1783 the treaty of Paris was signed, by which England admitted the independence of the United States and recognized the Great Lakes as our northern boundary, though it was not until 1796, after the ratification of Jay's treaty, that she abandoned some of the strongholds on our soil, including Fort Niagara.

WAR OF 1812.

It is foreign to the purpose of this article to discuss the causes, some of which had a bearing on this region, which led up to President Madison's proclamation of war between Great Britain and the United

States, known as the War of 1812, of which this immediate region, popularly called the Niagara frontier, felt the full force. In the fall of that year, four months after the declaration of war, Gen. Van Rensselaer established his camp near Lewiston (so called in honor of Gov. Lewis of New York), and collected an army to invade Canada. After one unsuccessful attempt he reached the Canadian shore, and by the time Gen. Brock had arrived from the mouth of the river to oppose him, was in possession of Queenston Heights. In endeavoring to recapture these and to retrieve the point of vantage that never should have been lost, Gen. Brock was killed. British reinforcements arriving from Niagara, the Americans were dislodged from the heights, defeated and many taken prisoners. Meanwhile, on the American side in full view of the battle, were some hundreds of American volunteers who basely refused to cross the river and aid their companions. At the foot of Queenston Heights an inscribed stone (set in place by the Prince of Wales in 1860) marks the spot where Brock fell and was buried; and on the heights above a lofty and beautiful column (the second one erected at this point, the first one having been blown up by a miscreant in 1840), stands as a monument of his country's gratitude. In the same year Gen. Alexander Smyth of Virginia issued his famous bombastic circular inviting everybody to join him at Black Rock, near Buffalo, and invade Canada from that point. Some five thousand men responded to his invitation, but Smyth having made himself a laughing-stock among his own people, the invasion was abandoned and the army dispersed

In the following year, 1813, the Americans captured Fort George on the Canadian shore near the mouth of the Niagara River and the village of Newark or Niagara. This is the oldest settlement in this section. It was for a time the residence of the Lieutenant Governor of Canada, and here in 1792 the first Parliament of Upper Canada held its session. Newark was burned by the Americans on their retreat, without reason, as the British claimed, and they immediately retaliated; for ten days later they surprised and captured Fort Niagara and burned every American village on the Niagara River, including Youngstown, Lewiston, Manchester (now Niagara Falls), Fort Schlosser, Black Rock, and Buffalo, spreading devastation along the American frontier. The year 1814 witnessed two battles in the vicinity of the Falls themselves, both on the Canadian side. Chippewa, a victory for the Americans, and Bridgewater or Lundy's Lane, claimed as a victory by both parties. The latter was one of the most remarkable conflicts recorded in history. Within sight of the Falls, in the glory of the light of a full moon, the opposing armies engaged in hand-to-hand conflict, from sun-down to midnight, when both sides, exhausted by their efforts, withdrew from the field. The British before dawn, and unopposed, re-occupied the battle ground, and on this alone rests their claim to victory. Later on the American army occupied Fort Erie, which they had shortly before wrested from the British and where they were besieged by them. From this Fort on the seventeenth of September, 1814, the Americans made that famous and successful sortie, which disbanded the British besiegers, this being the only case in history according to Lord Napier, where a besieging army was entirely defeated and disbanded by such a movement.

We necessarily omit all reference to many points along the river made famous by the exploits, the daring and often by the loss of life of the combatants in this war — points locally important in themselves but which have not risen to the dignity of that much abused word "history."

The Treaty of Ghent restored peace to both countries and to the inhabitants on their exhausted frontiers. Under this treaty, commissioners were appointed to locate the boundery line between Canada and the United States, already somewhat laxly provided for in the treaty of 1783. These commissioners agreed to run the boundery line along this frontier, through the middle of the Horse Shoe Falls and through the deepest channel of the River, both above and below them. Thus Navy Island fell to the share of the Canadians and Grand Island became American soil.

LAND TITLES.

We have already noted the cession of this region by the French to the English in 1763, and also the cession by the English of the eastern side of the river to the United States at the close of the revolutionary war, which joint occupation has never since been permanently disturbed. We also noted the cession by the Senecas to the English of the land on each side of the river and of the islands to Sir William Johnson and by him to the English crown.

A strip of land one mile wide along the American shore from Lake Ontario to Lake Erie had been exempted, when New York ceded the ownership of what is now the western portion of this State, to Massachusetts, which ownership New York subsequently re-acquired. Finally the Indians, who, in spite of their former cession to England, still claimed the ownership, ceded to New York, for $1,000 and an annuity of $1,500, their title to all the islands in the Niagara river. In order to get the title New York had previously acquired title from the Indians to the mile strip which had been alloted to America by the treaty of Ghent. The State of New York patented this mile strip to individuals commencing in the first decade of this century.

FAMOUS INCIDENTS.

Fort Niagara became a spot of national celebrity

in 1824. William Morgan, a resident of Batavia in this state, and a member of the Masonic Fraternity, threatened to disclose the secrets of that body in print. He was quietly seized and taken away from his home. He was traced in the hands of his abductors to Fort Niagara, where he is said to have been incarcerated in one of the cellars of the fort, and to this day "Morgan's dungeon" is one of the sights shown to visitors. He was never heard of after he entered the fort, and popular fancy says that he was taken from this dungeon by night and drowned in Lake Ontario. Several persons were subsequently tried for his murder, but no proof of their complicity in the matter, nor even of Morgan's death was produced. The principal episode in the famous anti-Masonic agitation of that period thus became a part of Niagara's local history.

In the same year Grand Island, which contains about eighteen thousand acres, was selected by Major M. M. Noah as the future home of the Jews of the New World. He proposed to buy the island, make of it a second Jerusalem, and within the sound of Niagara to build up an ideal community of wealth and industry. In 1825, acting as the Great High Priest of the Project, clad in sacerdotal robes, attended in procession by the civic and military authorities, local societies and a great concourse of people, with appropriate ceremonies, he laid the corner stone of his future City of Ararat on the altar of a Christian Church in

Buffalo. This corner stone was subsequently built into a monument at Whitehaven on Grand Island, opposite the village of Tonawanda. It is now in the possession of the Buffalo Historical Society. Major Noah's plan fell through, as the Patriarch of Jerusalem refused his sanction to the project.

THE PATRIOT WAR.

In 1837 occurred what is known as the Canadian Patriot War. While the agitation of the Patriots centered in Toronto, it kept the entire Niagara frontier on the Canadian side in a ferment for several months, and Navy Island became one of their rendezvous, a portion of the British troops being stationed at Chippewa. Without reference to the intrigues carried on along the frontier by the Canadian agitators with their American sympathizers, we deal only with the one important event known as the Caroline episode. It was openly charged that the Patriots were receiving substantial aid from the American side, not only from private individuals, but also by reason of the non-intervention of national and state authorities, when they knew that arms were being shipped and material assistance rendered from American soil. So bitter was the feeling on the part of the Britishers, that when the opportunity offered, it is not surprising that they made the most of it. A small steamer, the Caroline, had been chartered by Buffalo parties to run between that city, Navy Island where the insurgents were encamped, and

Schlosser Landing on the American shore. According to their statement it was a private enterprise, started to make money by carrying excursionists to the insurgents' camp; but according to the Canadian view, her real business was to convey arms and provisions to the insurgents. On the night of December 29 the Caroline lay at Schlosser's dock. The excitement had drawn large numbers of people here; all the hotels were filled, and some people had sought a night's lodging on the steamer itself. At midnight six boat loads of British soldiers, sent from Chippewa by Sir Allan McNab, silently approached the Caroline, boarded and captured her, turned off all on board, cut her moorings, set her on fire and towed her into the river. In the melée and exchange of shots, one man, Amos Durfee, was killed. The boat was burned to the waters edge and sank not far from where she had been cut adrift.

The affair caused intense excitement and was the source of long diplomatic correspondence, the British government assuming full responsibility for the claimed breaches of international law. One man, Alexander McLeod, was arrested and tried in this State for manslaughter and finally acquitted.

THE ERIE CANAL.

On October 26, 1825, a cannon boomed forth its greeting at Buffalo; a few seconds afterward another cannon a short distance down the River caught up the sound, and so on, cannon after cannon, cannon after cannon, down the Niagara River to Tonawanda, thence easterly to Albany, thence down the bank of the Hudson to New York City, transmitting the message that at the source of the historic Niagara River the waters of Lake Erie had been let into that just completed water-way—the Erie Canal.

THE FENIAN WAR.

From the time of the Patriot War, with the exception of the Fenian Outbreak in 1866, the history of this region has nothing to do with international war. The Fenian Outbreak, similar in its inception so far as its hostility to the existing government of Canada and a desire to aid the Irish cause of home-rule by inciting hostilities among England's colonies, was quickly suppressed. Of actual hostilities during that agitation there was but one occurrence, known as the battle of Ridgeway on the Canadian side in the vicinity of Buffalo, where the Fenians were defeated.

COMMERCIAL HISTORY.

In its commercially historic aspects, there stands out one important project in connection with Niagara Falls which has been broached by its advocates in public and in private, and especially in the halls of Congress for the past three quarters of a century. Although by international treaty, no war vessels are permitted on the upper lakes, in the line of Washington's famous aphorism, that "the best way to maintain peace is to be prepared for war," the advocates of a ship canal of a capacity large enough to float our largest vessels, connecting the Niagara River some two or three miles above the Falls with its quiet waters at Lewiston or below, have continued their agitations; and preliminary appropriations, and elaborate surveys—showing three or four routes—have been made by Congress at three different times. The project so far has made but little headway towards a successful consideration. Of its earliest commercial history, during the first years of the century, when private individuals bought the land from the State on account of its adjacent water power, and established here a village which they named Manchester,—of the first utilization of a portion of its enormous power in recent years and of the present stupendous power development now nearing completion, we cannot treat for lack of space. The enormous development of power and its electrical transmission with all that this will add to Niagara's future history are treated of elsewhere in this volume.

STATE RESERVATION AT NIAGARA.

In 1885, after some years of public agitation, the State of New York acquired Goat Island and the territory on the river bank adjacent to the Falls and for a half-mile above them, dedicating it by its ownership as free forever to the world. The Province of Ontario took a similar course on the Canadian side, so that from now on the Falls themselves and the adjacent lands, under the ownership of two friendly nations, are forever preserved from any real defacement of their scenery by commercial enterprises. The honor of first suggesting this preservation of the scenery has been claimed by many persons. But the first real suggestion, though made without details, came from two Scotchmen, Andrew Reed and James Matheson, who in 1835, in a volume describing their visit to the Congregational churches of this country, first broached the idea that Niagara should " be deemed the property of civilized mankind."

INDIAN LORE.

This region is rich in Indian lore and tradition which is Indian history) never yet thoroughly collected. Commencing far back when the Neuter nation, or more probably an earlier race*, dwelt hereabouts, they worshipped the Great Spirit of the Falls, their worship culminating annually in the sacrifice of the fairest maiden of the tribe to the Great Spirit of Niagara, sending her over the Falls in a white canoe laden with fruits and flowers; next, their inter-tribal wars ; later on the temporarily successful but ultimately inevitable futile attempt of the Neuter nation to maintain a neutral existence ; their use of Goat Island as the burying ground of their chiefs and warriors, and their adoration of the island because of such use ; their subsequent joining of the Iroquois to avoid total destruc-

---

*The Tuscaroras who live on the reservation near Lewiston are the descendants of the North Carolina tribe, who came to New York in 1712 and joined the confederacy of the Iroquois.

tion by them; later on their annihilation as a distinct tribe, the remnant that was left seeking refuge among the Hurons; their return after a lapse of nearly three-quarters of a century and their ultimate extinction, form an unwritten page of historic Niagara which will probably never be completed with the accuracy that its importance demands.

LOCAL HISTORY.

To later local history in different aspects, we can only refer; to the engineering triumphs in the various bridges that span this River and the attendant benefits to this region; to the famous achievements of Blondin and others who have crossed the gorge on a rope; to the trip made by the *Maid of the Mist* in 1861, under the guidance of Joel R. Robinson from Niagara to Lewiston—the only boat that has ever successfully done so—proving, so far as that portion of the river is concerned, what the courts have held, that the Niagara River throughout its entire length is a navigable stream; to men, who like Francis Abbot have associated their names with the Falls in one way, or like Capt. Webb, with the Rapids in another way; to the fall of Table Rock in 1850, showing to this generation the undermining process by which Niagara has cut the gorge; or to the numberless accidents which have annually occurred, some by accident, some intentionally.

Each of these in one way or another have tended to make history, and to point out lines of thought whose deductions must benefit future generations, and to all those which are necessarily blended with Niagara's history, we can but refer in this way.

Such, in outline, and with almost brutal brevity, is the foundation for that great work to which some master mind will some day devote its energies, and produce, to its own fame and to the benefit of international literature, a work whose pages shall contain events as yet imperfectly recorded and whose subject may be the words of our title, *Historic Niagara*.

FAC-SIMILE OF A VIEW OF NIAGARA FALLS BY
FATHER HENNEPIN.
(*From the Original Utrecht Edition, 1697*).

The Flora and Fauna of Niagara Falls
By David F Day.

THE traveler, who seeks for exhibitions of the grander forces of nature, will find his wishes abundantly gratified at Niagara. The fall of the waters of one of the greatest rivers of the world over a precipice of more than one hundred and fifty feet in height, and the constantly growing record of their power to channel through the enduring rock, will prove to him an absorbing, yet perplexing, subject for study. But the tourist, who takes enjoyment in the shadows of a forest, almost unchanged from its natural condition, in the stateliness and symmetry of individual trees, planted by the hand of Nature herself, in the beauty and fragrance of many species of flowers, growing without cultivation and in countless numbers, in the ever-varying forms and hues of foliage, and in the continually shifting panorama of the animated creation so near the scenes of human activity and occupation and yet so free from their usual effects, will find upon the borders of the river, within its chasm and on the islands, which hang upon the brink of the great cataract, an abundant gratification of his taste and an exhaustless field for study.

To such a person—to all, in fact, who realize how ennobling it is to the heart of man to be brought at times face to face with Nature, whether in her beauty or her sublimity—it must always be the source of profound satisfaction to know that by the wise and liberal policy of the State of New York and the Dominion of Canada, so large an area of country, contiguous to the river and the Falls, has been made a public property, and, placed forever beyond the reach of vandal hands, is now dedicated, for all time, to the highest and most exalted purposes.

Although in this volume a chapter has been devoted to the geology of Niagara, by one abundantly qualified for the task, nevertheless, for a proper presentation of the Natural History of the Falls and of the region of which it is the centre, a passing glance should here be bestowed upon the geological record of Goat Island and the river, within whose embrace it lies, to bring out more clearly the relation to it of its Fauna and Flora. For this purpose it is not necessary to explore the measureless periods of time in which the imagination of the geologist is accustomed to range at will. It is demonstrable that in a scientific sense the Island itself is of a trifling antiquity. In fact it would be difficult to point out in the western world any considerable tract of land more recent in its origin.

There is every evidence to believe that the Niagara River has excavated its enormous chasm since the close of the period known to geologists as the Glacial Age. Whether before the coming on of the Glacial Age the upper lakes were connected or not with Lake Ontario (a proposition which seems to be well received in the geological world), it seems very certain that thereafter Lake Erie, Lake Huron and Lake Superior sent their waters to the sea through an outlet which Lake Michigan then had into the Mississippi. A barrier not greater than fifty feet in height would suffice, even to-day, to reverse the current of Lake Erie and Lake Huron and compel the discharge of their contents into the Mississippi, either by re-opening the old, abandoned channel at the head of Lake Michigan or by forming a new one. The barrier, which was broken down at the time, when in fact the physical history of the Niagara River began, may be pointed out with reasonable certainty to-day. A ridge near the foot of Lake Erie, which at one time extended in an eastward and westward course, crossing the present channel of the Niagara River, was that barrier. On either side of the river it attains a height of sixty or seventy feet above the present level of Lake Erie. It is almost unnecessary to say that this barrier was of glacial origin—an immense moraine. From its base, on the northerly side, to the verge of the cliff at Lewiston and Queenston, where the cataract began its work of erosion, the surface of the underlying rock rises steadily. At the summit of the cliff at Lewiston and Queenston, it has an elevation of thirty-two feet above the present level of Lake Erie.

It is fair to assume that although the lake (or river), after its irruption through this barrier, spread widely, yet that the beginning of the excavation of the chasm at Lewiston was not long delayed.

Along the entire length of the river from Lake Erie to Lewiston and Queenston, the terraces, left by the river, as from time to time it deepened and narrowed its channel, may be easily recognized. Often they show evidence that they were formed at the bottom of the river before the chasm had been excavated, being very largely composed of water-worn stones and materials, brought and deposited by the river itself from more southerly localities.

Goat Island is of this origin. It is in fact a portion of such a terrace. In a single place upon the Island there is to be seen a small quantity of clay, possibly deposited by the glacier where it is found, but more likely to have been brought by the current of the river along with the other materials which make up the soil. Mixed with the soil of Goat Island and with that of the river terraces in other places, there may be seen an abundance of the half-decomposed remains of fluviatile and lacustrine Mollusca—shell-fish, univalve and bivalve, identical in species with those still living in the lake and river.

The period which has been employed by the river

in the excavation of the chasm, below the Falls, has, for more than half a century, been a most interesting study of the geologist. As early as 1841, Sir Charles Lyell, pre-eminent in his day as a geologist, from such data as he was then able to command, computed the time necessary for the work at no less than 35,000 years. Later geologists have sought, but unsucessfully, to reduce the period. When, however, the Island appeared above the river, substantially as it now is, presents a more difficult problem. But that the deposit of the materials, of which its soil is composed, began as soon as the irruption of the river through the moraine, at the foot of Lake Erie, was accomplished, can scarcely be doubted. That 35,000 years have passed, since the shells, found on the Island and in the terraces on either side of the river, were deposited, and that no specific difference is to be discovered, between them and their existing representatives and progeny, are facts full of interest to the evolutionist.

A calcareous soil, enriched with an abundance of organic matter, like that of Goat Island, would necessarily be one of great fertility. For the growth and sustentation of a forest, and of such plants as prefer the woods to the openings, it would far excel the deep and exhaustless alluvions of the Prairie States.

For the preservation of so large a part of the native vegetation of the Island, we must be thankful to the policy of its former owners, who, through so many

The Horse Shoe Falls from Canada—Looking towards the Three Sisters.

years, kept it mainly in the condition in which Nature left it. To the naturalist, the hand of cultivation is often the hand of devastation. It has happily been spared, to a large extent, from the ravage of the axe and plough, and from the still more complete spoliation which comes from the pasturage of horses and cattle. It would be very difficult to find within another territory, so restricted in its limits, so great a diversity of trees and shrubs—still more difficult to find, in so small an area, such examples of arboreal symmetry and perfection, as the Island has to exhibit.

From the geological history of the Island, as has thus been told, it would be inferred that it had received its Flora from the mainland. This, no doubt, is true. In fact the botanist is unable to point out a single instance of tree, or shrub, or herb, now growing upon the Island, not also to be found upon the mainland. But, as has been remarked, the distinguishing characteristic of its Flora is not the possession of any plant, elsewhere unknown, but the abundance of individuals and species, which the Island displays.

There are to be found in Western New York about one hundred and seventy species of trees and shrubs. Goat Island and the immediate vicinity of the river near the Falls can show of these no less than one hundred and forty.

Of our trees, producing conspicuous flowers, such as the Cucumber-tree (*Magnolia acuminata*), and the

Tulip-tree (*Liriodendron tulipifera*), there are but few specimens in the vicinity of the Falls. Abbe Provancher found the former growing at or near Clifton, and one magnificent specimen of the latter may be pointed out on Goat Island. In the re-forestation of the denuded portions of the Island due observance to the planting of these beautiful American trees should be had.

Four Maples are represented upon the Island:— *Acer saccharinum*, *A. rubrum*, *A. dasycarpum* and *A. spicatum*. The first of these, the Sugar-maple, is perhaps the most abundant tree upon the Island. Five species of Sumach (*Rhus*) grow upon the Island or along the margin of the river. Our native Plum (*Prunus Americana*) and two Cherries (*Prunus Virginiana* and *P. serotina*) belong either to the Island or the mainland, the latter, the Black-cherry of the lumberman, attaining upon the Island a wonderful development. Near the gorge of the river, on either side, but not upon the Island, the Crab-apple (*Pyrus coronaria*) abounds, diffusing in the early days of June its unequaled fragrance upon the air.

Three species of Thorn (*Cratægus coccinea*, *C. tomentosa* and *C. Crus-galli*), are to be met with upon Goat Island, adding in May and June, no small part to the floral magnificence of the season. Six species of Cornel, including the flowering Dog-wood (*Cornus florida*), two elders (*Sambucus Canadensis* and *S.*

pubens) and six Viburnums (*V. Opulus, V. acerifolium, V. pubescens, V. dentatum, V. nudum,* and *V. Lentogo*) either on the Island or the mainland, contribute greatly, in the spring and summer months, to enlarge and diversify the display.

To find the Sassafras one must go down along the river as far as the whirlpool. He will there meet with it, but not in profusion, on either side of the river. Our other native laurel, the Spice-wood (*Lindera Benzion*) is to be found handsomely represented on Goat Island.

Two species of Ash, the white and black, (*Fraxinus Americana* and *F. sambucifolia*) are among the trees of the Island, and are to be met elsewhere in abundance.

The only species of Linden or Bass-wood, which belongs to the vicinity, is the familiar one, *Tilia Americana*. It is plentiful upon the Island and of extraordinary size and beauty.

Of nut-producing trees the following occur :

The Butternut (*Juglans cinerea*), the Black walnut (*J. nigra*), the white Hickory (*Carya alba*), the hairy Hickory (*C. tomentosa*), the pignut Hickory (*C. porcina*), and the bitter Hickory (*C. amara*), the Beech (*Fagus ferruginea*), the Chestnut (*Castanea vulgaris*), the white Oak (*Quercus alba*), the post Oak (*Q. obtusiloba*), the Chestnut-oak (*Q. Muhlenbergii*), the Bur-oak (*Q. macrocarpa*), the dwarf Chestnut-oak (*Q. prinoides*), the red Oak (*Q. rubra*), the scarlet Oak (*Q. coccinea*), the Quercitron-oak (*Q. tinctoria*), and the Pin-oak (*Q. palustris*).

Two species of Elm (*Ulmus Americana* and *U. fulva*), three Birches (*Betula lenta, B. lutea* and *B. papyracea*), one Alder (*Alnus incana*), six native Willows (*Salix nigra, S. lucida, S. discolor, S. rostrata, S. petiolaris* and *cordata*), and four Poplars (*Populus tremuloides, P. grandidentata, P. monolifera* and *P. balsamifera v. candicans*), are embraced within the Sylva of Niagara.

Of the cone-bearing family the number of species is not as great as might be expected. They are only six, distributed in five genera, as follows:

The White-cedar (*Thuja occidentalis*), the most abundant of the evergreens at Niagara, the Red-cedar (*Juniperus Virginiana*), unfortunately disappearing, the Juniper (*J. communis*), the American Yew or Ground-hemlock (*Taxus baccata v. Canadensis*), the White-pine (*Pinus Strobus*), and the common Hemlock-spruce, (*Tsuga Canadensis*). The two last named species are not so plentiful upon the Island as their beauty demands. They should be at once and largely replanted.

Of the herbs, producing showy flowers, which are to be found upon the Island, the following may be mentioned, which by their profusion as well as beauty, make it in spring time and early summer, a natural flower-garden, wild indeed, but wonderfully beautiful:—

Our two Liverworts or Squirrel-cups (*Hepatica acutiloba* and *H. triloba*), scarcely distinguishable from one another, except by the leaf, but of an infinite variety of color.

The diœcious Meadow Rue (*Thalictrum dioicum*), more noticable because of the peculiar beauty of its foliage than its conspicuousness of flower. As graceful as a fern.

The wild Columbine (*Aquilegia Canadensis*), to be found on the Island, yet more abundantly along the chasm, where it displays its elegant blossoms of scarlet and gold, far beyond the reach of the most venturesome.

The May Apple (*Podophyllum peltatum*), a plant singular both in flower and leaf, but beautiful and always arresting attention.

The Blood-root (*Sanguinaria Canadensis*), a plant lifting up its large, clear white flower and its solitary leaf in the early days of spring.

Squirrel-corn and Dutchman's breeches (*Dielytra Canadensis* and *D. cucullaria*). Strange plants, but of great gracefulness and beauty. Abundant on the Island early in May. The former species, rich with the odor of hyacinths.

Of the spring-flowering *Cruciferæ*, to be found upon the Island, the following deserve to be mentioned as notable for their abundance and beauty :— The Crinkle-root (*Dentaria diphylla*), the Spring-cress

(*Cardamine rhomboidea, v. purpurea*), and the Rockcress (*Arabis lyrata*).

As many as four violets abound upon the Island and its vicinity, adding their charms to the beauty of the month of May—*Viola cucullata, V. rostrata, V. pubescens,* and *V. Canadensis,* the last, remarkable among the American species, for its fragrance as well as gracefulness.

The Spring-beauty (*Claytonia Caroliniana*), the large, native Cranesbill (*Geranium maculatum*), the Virginian Saxifrage (*Saxifraga Virginiensis*, the two Mitre-worts (*Tiarella cordifolia* and *Mitella diphylla*), the spreading Phlox (*P. divaricata*), the creeping Greek Valerian (*Polemonium reptans*), now rather rare, the American Dog-tooth Violet or Adder's-tongue (*Erythronium Americanum*), the large-flowered Bell-wort (*Uvularia grandiflora*), the Indian Turnip (*Arisæma triphylla*, and the two Trilliums (*T. grandiflorum* and *T. erectum*), add largely to the spring contingent of attractive and conspicuous plants.

Later in the season, one may find the shrubby St. John's Wort (*Hypericum Kalmianum*), and one of the most graceful species of Lobelia (*L. Kalmii*), each rejoicing in a damp situation, and each, quite probably, discovered at the Falls, by Bishop Kalm, nearly a century and a half ago, and introduced by him, from that locality, to the notice of the botanical world. The name of the discoverer of these interesting plants is worthily commemorated in those which the great Linnæus bestowed upon them.

The summer time brings forward many attractive forms—the Grass of Parnassus (*Parnassia Caroliniana*), the Painted-Cup (*Castilleia coccinea*), an occasional lily, an orchid or two, but of no great beauty, the Hare-bell (*Campanula rotundifolia*), and a large array of annuals.

Nor is the autumnal Flora of Goat Island uninteresting. Golden-rods (*Solidago* sp.), Sun-flowers (*Helianthus* sp.), Star-flowers (*Aster* sp.), the Downy Thistle (*Cnicus discolor*), and, at last, the triumph of October and the dying year, the shorn Gentian (*Gentiana detonsa*), its graceful blossoms as blue as the summer skies.

In the region of the Falls, but not upon Goat Island itself, some plants of great beauty have been detected. Below the Whirlpool, two species of Bluets or Innocence (*Houstonia cærulea* and *H. purpurea*), are to be observed, the rare *Liatris cylindracea*, *Apocynum androsæmifolium*, the orange-colored Milkweed (*Asclepias tuberosa*), the Fire-lily (*Lilium Philadelphicum*), the large, yellow Lady's slipper (*Cypripedium pubescens*), the beautiful, low-growing Morning Glory (*Convolvulus spithamæus*), and wild Roses, as fragrant as beautiful.

The ferns of Goat Island and the region of the Falls are numerous. Among them may be mentioned :—The Ostrich-fern (*Onoclea Struthiopteris*), the Sensitive-fern (*O. sensibilis*), the Royal-fern (*Osmunda regalis*), the Interrupted-fern (*O. interrupta*), the Cinnamon-fern (*O. cinnamomea*), the Bladder-fern (*Cystopteris bulbifera*), Shield-ferns, of various species (*Aspidium Noveboracense, A. Thelypteris, A. spinulosum, A. cristatum, A. Goldianum, A. marginale, A. Lonchitis*), and the Christmas-fern (*A. achrostichoides*), the Beech-fern (*Phegopteris Dryopteris*), only found at the Devil's Hole, the Walking-fern (*Camptosorus rhyzophyllus*), four Spleen-worts (*Asplenium Trichomanes, A. ebeneum*, abundant at Lewiston, *A. achrostichoides* and *A. Filix-fœmina*), scarcely to be excelled in grace by any species, two Cliff-brakes (*Pellæa gracilis* and *P. atropurpurea*), the Common-brake, world-wide in its distribution (*Pteris aquilina*), the American Maidenhair (*Adiantum pedatum*), and the common Polypody (*Polypodium vulgare*), peering, in many places, over the edge of the chasm into the depths below.

Of the Fauna of Niagara very much cannot be said. All the larger Mammalia, which abounded in the region whilst it was still the possession of the red man, have long since disappeared. It seems almost as though they could never have resorted, habitually, to Goat Island. The access to it of the elk, the red deer, the bear, the panther, the lynx, the fox and the wolf, common enough in the neighborhood, must always have been difficult, and their return to the mainland almost impossible. At the present time the quadrupeds inhabiting the Island are probably only three, the Black-squirrel, the Red-squirrel and the Striped Squirrel or Chipmunk. These may be seen, almost any spring or summer day, disporting themselves, without regard to the presence of man, in their leafy coverts.

The birds affecting the Island and the gorge are not to be distinguished, in species, from those of the mainland. But, as would be expected, environment makes some species rare and others plentiful. The Robin (*Turdus migratorious*), the Oriole (*Icterus Baltimore*), the Blue-bird (*Sialia Wilsonii*) and the Goldfinch (*Carduelis tristis*), find so much of their food supply in door yards and cultivated land, that they are to be seen less frequently upon the Island or within the gorge, than elsewhere in the neighborhood. On the other hand, birds of the deep and silent woods, like the Vireos, Wilson's Thrush (*Turdus fuscescens*), the Wood-thrush (*Turdus mustelinus*), and the Cat-bird, (*Mimus Carolinensis*), are almost always to be seen and heard in the vicinity of the Falls or river.

Birds of the crow family, such as the common Crow, the Purple Grackle and the Blue-jay were probably, at one time, plentiful; but they are now rarely seen, except as they are passing over from one side of the river to the other. Our common hawks may be included in the same remark.

Summer or winter, numerous gulls may be seen hovering over the river, between its high banks, below the Falls.

Late in the autumn, after other birds have taken their flight, in the thick spray of the Red-cedars, great flocks of Cedar-birds (*Amphelis cedrorum*) are to be noticed, feeding socially upon the plentiful sweet berries of the tree. Probably they remain until the supply of food is exhausted.

The Bald-headed Eagle (*Haliætus leucocephalus*) was once a frequenter of the region of the cataract, but is now seldom seen. Probably he has learned to be wary and not unnecessarily to expose himself to the aim of the collecting naturalist. But, however that may be, without doubt the waters below the Falls were once a favorite resort to him. He was a devourer of fish, and, although powerful of claw and pinion, he did not disdain to save his strength by feeding upon such as had been killed or stunned in their passage over the Falls.

Of the birds of our region, which seem to fear the presence of man, and therefore retire to the unfrequented woods, it may be said that they are really plentiful in the shady nooks and recesses with which the gorge of the river abounds. The naturalist, who would wish to make them a study, can do so, satisfactorily, if he will but enter the woods at the Whirlpool or at Foster's Flat and patiently and quietly await their appearance. It is hardly possible that such a retiring species as the Indigo-bird (*Cyanospiza cyanea*) will fail to reward his watchfulness, or that a Scarlet Tanager (*Pyranga rubra*) will not soon flash like a meteor before his eyes. Likely enough the Kingfisher (*Ceryle Alcyon*), will leave his silent perch and with a harsh cry dart down upon his scaly prey. Here, where the thick leaves make a twilight, even at mid-day, the attentive ear of the student of our birds will listen, with delight, to the bell-like notes of the Wood-thrush, or to the sweet cadences of the Cat-bird's real song.

AS : IT : RUSHES : BY.

By E. S. MARTIN

THE great North-west has two ways of reaching tide-water. It filters down the Mississippi, losing impetus as it goes southward, until, too much enervated to dig itself a channel, it rolls sluggishly on between artificial levees and slips unobtrusively into the Gulf by a dozen different passages. The farther south it goes the more irresponsible it becomes and the more need it has of assistance. To get it safely emptied is a constant care, calling for perpetual labor and congressional appropriations. At the least neglect it slops lazily over, and settles down on the surrounding country.

How differently it comes East, navigating the great western lakes one after another, and finally crowding impetuously into the Niagara River and over its precipice with a roar and a jarring crash, and then out through Ontario and the swift St. Lawrence to the Ocean! Journeying southward it blends imperceptibly with the region it traverses, so that it is hard to say where the west leaves off and the south begins. But it drops down upon the East with an enormous plunge that leaves no doubt of the whereabouts of the line of demarcation. Beyond Niagara is the West. Here the East begins, equal to the West in energy and vim, but different The West never merges with the East as it does with the South. It comes to Niagara in overwhelming force and thunders at its gates, and then rolls off North-easterly and out through the British provinces. It asks nothing of man except to be let alone. It has dug its own channel with its own tools, and formed itself a basin of ample size to hold it. It is responsible, self-reliant, fully able to take care of itself, and ever ready to do any odd jobs that offer as it surges along. It seems to gather energy from the invigorating influences that meet it in its progress.

Colonel Ingersoll came to Niagara one day and looked at the tribute of the great Northwest as it surged by, and said : " Niagara Falls is a dangerous place."

There was disparagement in the Colonel's tone, and disparagement is something to which Niagara is not much used. Whatever native it was that heard him stared and asked : " Do you mean the hackmen ? "

" No ! " said the eminent orator. " I mean those great rushing waters. There is nothing attractive to me in them. They are really dangerous. There is so much noise, so much tumult. It is simply a mighty force of nature, one of those tremendous powers which is to be feared for its danger."

The native's eyebrows went up at that. It is true enough that the Niagara River is not one that a cautious person would care to navigate, particularly above the Falls, but the Colonel, though not anchored to anything, was at least on firm land. The reflection suggested itself, that he had imperfectly diagnosed his own sensations, and that his dissatisfaction, which was obviously genuine, really sprung from the traditional disagreement of two of a trade. How could an orator be edified by a tone besides which his own best utterance was but a squeak? To make impressions is the orator's business, not to receive them. But at Niagara, Nature does the talking and has her say out, and man's part is to listen and to digest. It was a high compliment that the great talker paid to the river by his instinctive disapproval, and perfectly consistent with his point of view were his continuing remarks:

"What I like in Nature is a cultivated field where men can work in the free, open air; where there is quiet and repose, not turmoil, strife, tumult, fearful roar, or struggle for mastery. I do not like the crowded, stuffy workshop where life is a slavery and drudgery, where men are slaves. Give me the calm, cultivated land of waving grain, of flowers, of happiness."

So spoke the man of super-abundant energy, not unnaturally preferring scenes that seem to require some stirring up to those where all the requisite agitation comes ready furnished to hand. It is true that to the professional regulator, Niagara bristles with discouragement. There is comparatively little left there for man to do. To keep his hands off and let Nature take her course is the chief boon that is asked of him. But it is about the last place in the world to be compared to a stuffy workshop where men are slaves. Indeed the very pith of its contrast to the " cultivated land of waving grain " lies in the absence here of conspicuous signs of human labor. Work was traditionally imposed upon man for his sins. Even if the natural man is not rightfully lazy, he is at least entitled to love leisure, and prefer the minimum of toil. Surely Niagara is fit to refresh his jaded spirit. If he sighs at the foot of the pyramids to think of the vast industry that was the cost of their construction, he is conversely entitled to exult at the resistless might of the Niagara River emptying its floods into its self-chiseled gorge. Only the planets wandering in their courses, harnessed to the sun, are so fit to stir an exultation of repose. Laborious man sits on our river's brink and meditates on the great spectacle of labor saved. The Falls just go themselves. Within the memory of man it has never been found needful even in the dryest times to operate them by artificial means. In sight or out of sight there is no apparatus for pumping water back into Lake Erie to keep the cataract going. Neither has it ever been found necessary to dam the lake to keep the water from running out, or to bail it out to keep it from running over. Nature has done everything. The lake is always full, the river never ceases to drain it. The precipice that the torrent goes over is not absolutely permanent or changeless, but like the rest of the apparatus it takes care of itself, asking nothing of man but to stand from under when its features shift.

The great lesson of Niagara is to maintain a respectful attitude towards Nature. She is irresistible; not to be thwarted, not to be turned aside. It is our affair to study her courses, to get out of her way when she wants the whole road, and to make her do our work by the simple expedient of making our desires consistent with her methods.

In this feature of the Falls lie their special adaptation to be gazed upon by young persons who have just entered the married state and assumed the more serious burdens of life. It is not accident that brings the newly married to Niagara. It is instinct. It is good for them to be here, and some subtle influence has taught them to know it. Seeking for entertainment not to be laboriously won, but of a sort that stimulates the faculties while it promotes reflection, they find it here. The river entertains them. It speaks to them in continuous discourse without exacting any reply. It distracts their attention gently from one another, which is a kindness, and when they speak together it prevents alien ears from overhearing what they say. It is uniformly kind to them—so long as they hug the bank—and then it gives them so many useful points for the shaping of their future destinies! It teaches them to let things slide when opposition will do no good. It stands to them for the resistless stream of life which sweeps us all over its falls first or last, so that it pays us to float tranquilly while we may and not mar so brief a passage with altercation. The individuality of so impetuous a flood can hardly fail to make its impression on them, suggesting that every individuality, even that of a married woman, has a right to its own development, and comes swifter and safer to a tranquil haven if left reasonably free to follow out its natural course.

But only dense men bully their wives anyway, and possibly such men are too impervious to instruction to gather the wisdom of Niagara as it rushes by. But its wisdom is always there for those who can seize it, and for all coming time its banks promise to be trod by men and women who have need at least to try.

The Utilization of Niagara's Power.
By Coleman Sellers, E.

FOR the first time in the history of Niagara Falls, attractions other than those furnished by nature are offered; not only to the mere pleasure seeker, but to the scientific world generally, in the attempt that is now being made to utilize some small portion of the power of the great cataract on a scale that is vast compared to all previous attempts at such utilization. This is to be done not by diminishing the beauty of the Falls, but by adding to what would otherwise attract the visitor to the place, the visible progress of a gigantic engineering enterprise that has no precedent in the civilized world or that can be compared to any of the other similar works of man in the results that may flow from the venture.

"What is the power of Niagara Falls?"

One fantastic computation, perhaps reliable, sets it down comparatively as being so great that if all the coal mined in the world each day should be burned to make steam, it would barely suffice to operate pumping machinery, to pump back the water from the lower river to supply what passes from Lake Erie into Lake Ontario at the Falls of Niagara. The difference of level between the still water above the Rapids and the River at the base of the Falls is about 216 feet. If we could with certainty determine just how much water per second passes the Falls, knowing the difference of level, every cubic foot per second would represent theoretically about 26 H. P., or if used to operate water wheels of 75 per cent. efficiency, each foot per second would be worth in power about 18 H. P. Unfortunately the whole head cannot be used. The mills on the banks below the Falls which are fed by the hydraulic canal use only 90 to 100 feet fall, or even less, and all the water that passes through such wheels gives power due to the fall used, and the remaining fall is at present wasted so far as its power is concerned. The work being done by the Cataract Construction Company for the Niagara Falls Power Company, whereby the power is to be developed above the American Rapids is based upon power that is obtainable by means of a tunnel for a tail race, the hydraulic slope of which leaves, with certainty, only about 140 feet available as a working head, and every cubic foot of water per second must be made to yield not less than 12 H. P.

In the Census Report of 1880, two large folio volumes were devoted to the water powers of the United States, and that of Niagara Falls is credited with a theoretical value of 5,878,100 H. P., representing in fuel consumption (at three pounds of coal per horse power per hour) about 211,611 tons of coal per day. The mills already located on the bank of the stream and fed by the hydraulic canal take from the Falls at present about 6,000 H. P., so that 200,000 H. P. more may be taken for man's use and leave 5,678,100 H. P. to be represented by the stream that will still pour over the crest of the Falls. The water to be taken represents an insignificant amount as compared with the whole torrent; in fact the daily fluctuation of the stream, owing to the action of the wind and other causes, while seeming to make little change in the water level of the upper river, still causes a far greater increase or diminution from time to time in the water passing over the crest than will possibly occur continuously by the abstraction of all the power that can be utilized by man.

To meet the demand for some reliable information as to what is proposed by the Niagara Falls Power Company, the main features of the enterprise will be given so far as they can be stated in advance of the actual completion of the works themselves, which are being erected to permit extension in accordance with the progress of the arts during the time of erection, and to meet the wants of those who will seek the neighborhood of the Falls as an advantageous location for mechanical, chemical and metallurgical industries.

Beyond this local supply, time alone can solve the question of just how far the power of Niagara Falls can be carried profitably. What is being done in preparing for long distance transmission is in perfect harmony with the use of the power at the Falls, and many cities of the State may soon share with Buffalo the benefits of cheap power electrically transmitted from Niagara.

The chief objects of interest connected with the new development of power at Niagara Falls are: the tunnel, now finished for 7,000 feet of its length; the main canal to carry water to the wheels; the excavation that is being made to receive the ten water wheels each of 5,000 H. P., which will generate the electricity by which to transmit power to a distance or to works near by; and the extensive establishment of the Niagara Falls Paper Co., the first to anticipate the new development and to risk, before the completion of the tunnel, the erection of an industrial plant that will at the outset use 3,000 H. P. generated by three separate wheels, with the capability of extending to six or seven thousand horse power; all of the wheels required for this establishment, designed and built in America, being under the personal control of the paper company.

The tunnel is a remarkable piece of engineering work, over a mile and a quarter long, the upper end lying more than 150 feet below the inlet canal, and thence sloping gradually towards the lower river where its discharge portal is visible a short distance below the Upper Suspension Bridge adjacent to the Government Reservation. The cross-section of this tunnel is

INLET CANAL AND NIAGARA RIVER.

of horse-shoe form, and is lined with brick throughout, the sides and roof being of the best quality of hard burnt brick, the concave floor or invert being paved with vitrified brick of great endurance. It is without curve in its entire length of 7,000 feet but its slope is not entirely uniform, being at the rate of 4 feet per 1,000 at the upper end, and the lower half sloping approximately at the rate of 7 feet to the 1,000 towards the mouth, where for some few hundred feet the floor slopes still more rapidly and is plated on the bottom and sides with steel, forming a wavelike curve that brings the extreme end a number of feet below the mean water level of the river. The back water standing in the tunnel at the mouth presents a water cushion to the outgoing stream as it leaves the tunnel and passes the open cut beyond the portal. An hydraulic gradient of seven feet to the thousand has been assumed as necessary to give the required velocity to the out-going water, hence the tunnel in its length of 7,000 feet already built consumes practically about 49 feet of the total difference of level between the upper and the lower river.

The nature of the rock through which the great tunnel was driven necessitated careful support of the roof and side walls by strong timbers, with a final lining of brick of sufficient thickness to insure durability. During the progress of this work, careful supervision of the hydraulic cement used, resulted in a structure in which the joints are as strong or stronger than the very excellent quality of bricks used in the lining. This was proven whenever it became necessary to cut through the walls to make lateral connections, the hard brick yielding more readily than the cement.

To obtain a comparative estimate of the durability of the building material used in the various parts of the work, numerous specimens of cement mixtures, as well as the bricks and stones required were subjected to the action of a sand blast, peculiarly arranged, so that a comparison was made of the ability of the material to stand attrition was tested by the projection of a given weight of sand driven under uniform pressure of blast, in often repeated trials, carefully weighing the specimen between each blast to determine the amount of material removed by the attrition of the sand. Before this test was adopted as reliable a succession of experiments demonstrated that with uniform material treated uniformly, a uniform amount of wear was shown to occur—as for example, in applying the sand blast test under the same conditions to various qualities of plate glass.

Without going into the detail of these experiments or giving the actual results, it is to be understood that the experiments so tried enabled the engineers to arrange the material in the progressive scale as to durability, also to confirm, with exactness, their judgment as to what mixtures of sand and cement, and with what treatment the condition equivalent to the strength of granite or brick or any other material to be united had been obtained. The tests so applied were conclusive as to the standing quality of each material and the method in which it was used in all cases. The adoption of vitrified brick for those places liable to be subjected to the greatest wear was warranted by the fact that such bricks stand at the top of the list of the materials used, resistiug the sand blast and therefore well fitted to resist any wearing action of sand or other material rapidly driven through the tunnel by the speed of the current.

The Power House on the west bank of the great canal is to be built of stone in harmony with the stone work of the walls of the canal itself, and lined with enamelled brick. The steel roof trusses of over 60 feet span rest upon steel posts that serve to carry the girders to sustain an electric traveling crane of 50 tons capacity. At the north end of the Power House a massive stone building of much greater width will form a prolongation to the north with an L extension eastward up to the edge of the main canal. This L and the extension of the Power House, forming the entrance front of the building, will present gable ends to the east and west. To the left of the entrance archway, the offices, four stories in height, will be located wholly in the L, while to the right, including the archway, the whole height of the Power House to which it is attached consists of one large room in which the 50-ton traveling crane commands the entire floor. An arched portal or main doorway of great height forms the entrance vestibule. Cars loaded to the limit permissible on the railroad can pass through this vestibule and then through a lower arch into the main Power House, where the load can be handled by the traveling crane. Over this second doorway, which in summer will be closed with iron grill work and in winter by doors, the archstones radiate fan-like to the roof of the main vestibule, and in the centre of these radiating archstones will be displayed as a medallion the semblance of the seal of the Company, designed by Frederick McMonnies, the American Sculptor. It represents the Indian chief Ni-a-ga-ra standing in his canoe, paddle in hand, shooting the rapids. The circular border is alternately the Muscalonge, the King-fish of the river, and the prevailing fossil shells of the Niagara group, *delthyis Niagarensis*. A doorway through the left wall of the vestibule gives entrance to the offices which occupy the four-story building on the canal, and also gives access to visitors who, passing the ticket office, can by an easy flight of stairs gain a platform level with the second story of the office building and thence by a second short flight of steps gain a bridge that crosses the great end room of the power station. From this bridge a view can be obtained of the electrical generators and of the various machinery required to effect the transformations from the alternating current of high potential to currents suited to the various uses, with the capability of delivery in just such quantity and force of current as may be required for the purposes to which electricity can be applied.

The electric generators in the Power House will of themselves show perhaps little that is especially attrac-

202   THE UTILIZATION OF NIAGARA'S POWER

tive, either as to massive proportions or intricate and curious machinery, but they will be wonderful for their simplicity, and the thoughtful visitor will be interested to know that each of the 80 odd thousand pounds of steel to be seen rapidly revolving like gigantic spinning tops is perhaps delivering a current of ten or twenty thousand volts pressure directly by cables that are concealed beneath the floor of the Power House, and

INTERIOR OF TUNNEL.

thence carried into an underground space below the bridge upon which the visitor will stand. Nearby will be seen the switch-boards with all the dangerous conductors entirely concealed from view. The operators handling the distributing devices will do so by means of silk cords attached to the various levers and other devices that must be moved to effect the distribution of the current.

In this room will be arranged all those instruments that will enable the electricians in charge to know exactly what is occurring at every part of the electrical system. Every centre of distribution, whether it is nearby or a hundred miles away, will be in direct communication and visibly record its condition to guide the operators in this Power House. There the currents can be controlled and the speed of the wheels regulated to suit the conditions required. Massive resistance coils will be provided to enable any one of these 5,000 H. P. generators to exhaust its entire power in heat or be instantly switched into the line requiring the additional supply.

From the Power House underground conduits will extend, in which on insulated benches on either side will be arranged all the distributing conductors, and through the main conduit will be passed an electric car upon which the linemen can ride between wire screens that protect them from the dangerous currents between which they pass, and yet allow every portion of the line, brilliantly illuminated by the passing car, to be inspected with absolute safety. Arrangements will be made whereby the current can be deflected from one side of the conduit to the other in order that access may be given for attachments or changes at any point of the line. The extension of this conduit will be first through the ground owned by the company, and thence on a smaller scale through Tonawanda to Buffalo, or a pole line similar to those in use in long distance transmissions in Europe will be erected.

It is the intention of the Company to employ a current of high potential and to so protect its transmission as to make it absolutely safe to human life and absolutely reliable in its continuity to those manufacturers at a distance who, renting the power, must feel that the supply can be relied upon. In no single case will any one machine or device be depended upon for power or for transmission; always spare machinery in excess of the actual need will be provided to permit stoppage for alterations or repairs.

Electricity has been adopted as the means of distributing the power from the central stations as promising the least loss of power, and the minimum cost in devices for its transmission. Compressed air may be used where advantageous.

When the Power House is finished to its ultimate length of over 400 ft., the greatest interest will centre in the ten great generators, each of 5,000 H. P., and each driven by a separate water wheel system. From the inspecting bridge, looking south along the building at intervals of about 40 ft. on the east wall towards the canal, that is to the left of the observer, machinery will be seen that is placed to operate the sluice gates which are used to partly regulate the water admitted to the wheels, or when need be, to shut off the whole supply. The actual regulation of the speed of the wheels will be effected at the wheels themselves by balanced gates which control the amount of water escaping from them, not by regulating the admission of water to the wheels. The amount of water required for each wheel is about 25,000 cubic ft. per minute, flowing to the wheels through channels from the main canal, each 17 ft. deep by 14 ft. wide, walled up of dressed stone with an average depth of water of about 12 ft. The position of these channels will be indicated by the gate machinery only, as otherwise they are hidden from view, beneath the floor Ten such channels are devoted to the Power House, while at suitable intervals on the main canal many other channels of similar size are provided for future use. Two gateways arranged with similar operating machinery to that in the Power House will control the admission of water to the long canal which feeds the Niagara Falls Paper Company's extensive works.

Weeds, grass and floating matter that might pass into the wheels and obstruct them are prevented from entering the inlet channels by means of racks or iron gratings, which are located at the mouth of each one of the entrance canals and arranged in such manner as

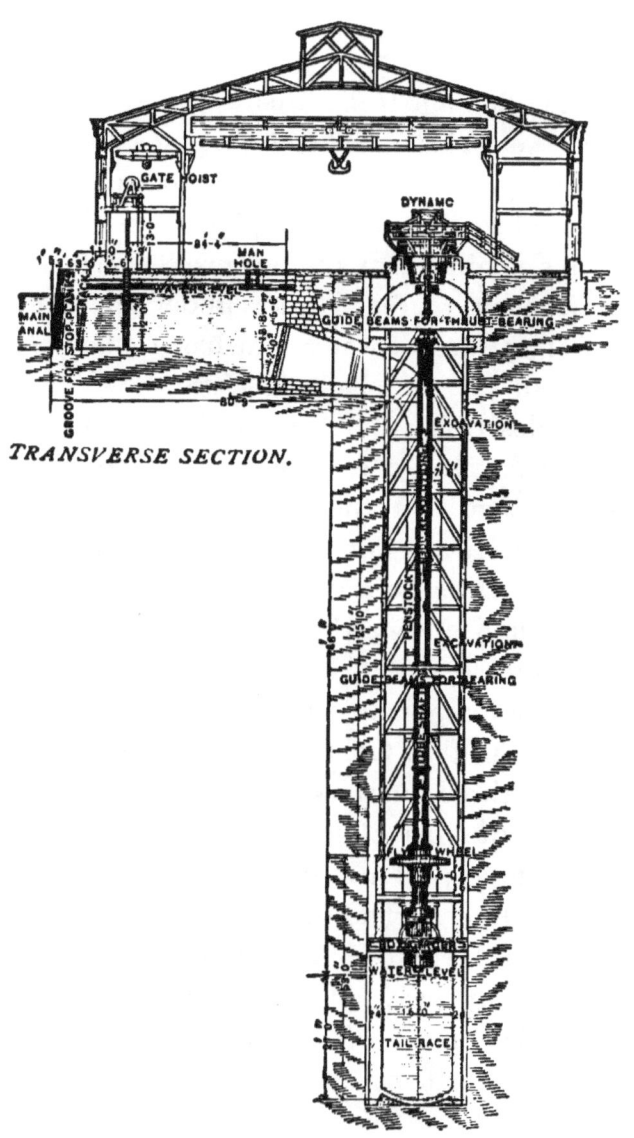

TRANSVERSE SECTION.

Transverse Sketch Showing Inlet from Main Canal.

to admit the floatage to be easily raked off and the water-way kept clear. The sluice gates already mentioned to roughly govern the water that passes to the wheels are of steel moving in planed cast iron guides, and resting against sets of loose rollers which permit easy movement of each gate under the enormous pressure of 75 tons of water that has to be restrained when closed.

Before describing the wheels that are to be used in the Power House it may be well to call attention to the fact that the conditions controlling the use of Niagara Falls for motive power are peculiar. The land on the American side of the river is a vast plain extending for miles in every direction. The Niagara River below Buffalo flows through this plain, a broad, comparatively quiet stream, breaking into rapids at the head of Goat Island, and from thence for a distance of three-quarters of a mile, the foaming torrent falling a number of feet reaches the crest of the fall to take its leap of 160 feet into the narrow gorge of the lower river. The deep cut below the Cataract into which this torrent pours has been formed by the gradual wearing away of the rocks of the Niagara group, as the breast of this mighty barrier has for ages past crept little by little towards its present site. The point where the Niagara Falls Power Co. must take the water from the still pool above the rapids is a mile and a quarter from the gorge below the Falls at its nearest point. The appurtenances of manufacturing are thus far removed from the Falls and its scenery. To develop power on the shore of the upper river, the water from wheels located in deep pits will be carried away through the seven thousand feet of tunnel that passes under the City of Niagara Falls, as already mentioned, and this tunnel is expected to develop 100,000 horse power with wheels that operate under an average of from 136 to 140 ft. head. In ordinary locations where natural differences of level in land exist, a water course raised above extensive plains available for building factories or mills, water wheels of any kind convenient for the purpose may be located close to the machinery that is to be driven, and the choice of the kind of wheel to be used is less restricted than in the present case. In California the simple and efficient Pelton wheel, so often mentioned as suitable for Niagara Falls, finds conditions exactly suited to its use, with unlimited space for its application.

Any wheel, however, with horizontal axis, buried 150 feet underground in restricted space, will need transmitting gearing and shafts or belts to carry the power to where it is to be used above, unless the driven machinery can be located in excavated chambers below. Many kinds of water wheels, such as the ordinary overshot, undershot, and other wheels revolving on horizontal axes, can only be used in the positions for which they are designed, while the modern turbines may be operated either vertically or horizontally, and in many cases the wheel with the vertical axis presents peculiar advantages. In the present case, considering the great amount of power required at once, with perhaps a market for over 50,000 horse power in the city of Buffalo alone, units of 5,000 horse power have been adopted after a most careful study of the subject in this country and through the International Niagara Commission in Europe. The water wheels for each unit are made in pairs on one vertical shaft; the water enters the wheel case between the two wheels from a vertical penstock made of steel $7\frac{1}{2}$ feet diameter. The constant water pressure in the penstock due to the head of about 136 feet serves to support the entire weight of all revolving parts, viz: weight of the wheels, the vertical shaft and the revolving parts of the generator that is to be driven by the wheel.

The great steel shaft upon which these wheels are placed is solid and of from 11 to 12″ diameter in some portions of its length, the solid parts occurring where journals are needed at intervals to steady the vertical shaft on fixed bearings; the shaft in the long intervals between the bearings is increased in diameter and made hollow for lightness, the hollow part of the shaft being formed of carefully rolled tubing, without any riveted vertical seams, so as to give the required strength and rigidity with diminished weight, lessening by the stiffness of the tubular shaft the number of supporting bearings that would otherwise be required for a shaft of uniform diameter so employed.

The mechanical problem to be solved in this case is very like that of a steam-ship where the motive power in the form of an engine, say 5,000 horse power, delivers that power through a long horizontal shaft to the propeller at the stern of the vessel, with the difference that at Niagara the engine is represented by the water wheels and the propeller by the revolving part of the generator, and the connecting shaft which is horizontal in the steamship is vertical in the case of the Niagara power. The arrangement of the machinery as adopted reduces the friction to the minimum as all the revolving parts, the water wheels, the vertical shaft and the revolving portions of the dynamo are all supported on a vertical axis and conditioned like a top spinning on water, the whole weight of the revolving mass being carried by the hydraulic pressure of the column of water that gives power to the wheels.

•The accurate governing of the speed of the machinery is a problem that has received the most careful attention and is in this case, met by the use of devices that have established their reliability by long service in Switzerland, where the wheels for Niagara were designed. To effect this comparatively accurate maintenance of speed requires a fly wheel as part of the system, this fly wheel being needed to prevent the accession or loss of speed when work suddenly varies. Fortunately in the present case the fly wheel capacity is obtained in the weight of the revolving part of the generator and that part alone will be seen in the operation of the generators in the Power House. Near to each generator will be located the governing machinery, which, though seemingly complicated, is nevertheless simple in its operation. The weight of the revolving part must be great enough in each case and the speed per second sufficient to insure over 18 millions of foot pounds of work to be stored in the revolving mass, resisting by inertia any sudden increase or decrease of the speed and permitting time for the governing machinery to move the gates that control the water escaping from the wheels below. The balls of the revolving governor, very similar to that used upon a steam engine, do not directly control the gates themselves, but control the powerful actuating machinery that continues to act only so long as a difference or variation of speed occurs in the rate of rotation of the governor balls, and ceases to act when these balls are revolving at their normal speed.

To insure the best results the specifications furnished to the builders of the machinery, required physical tests of strength so high as to deter some manufacturers from bidding, and in construction the high tests have been rigidly adhered to with the most satisfactory results. Where any doubt existed as to the kind of material to employ, preference has been given to that which would put the durability beyond any doubt. This is particularly the case in regard to the water-wheels themselves. The design was made with the expectation of using the best quality of cast iron, but from excessive caution, the order was issued that they should be made of bronze of the same quality as is used in the heavy propellers for steam ships. This adoption of bronze was on account of the failure of many of the cast iron wheels under a head of only 90 to 100 feet in use at Niagara, but the designers of the wheels for the Cataract Construction Co. hold that the failure of such wheels was due to the form of the blades and not to the material, and instanced wheels made of cast iron working under very much greater head and without any appreciable wear when properly proportioned. Bronze, however, was adopted at a very great increase of cost to render failure from any cause impossible so far as the wheels are concerned. The tests of material used in the construction was followed by the inspectors, from the mills to the manufacturing establishment making the wheels and other machinery, with the most careful precision and rigid adherence to the requirements of the specification.

Out of the seeming chaos of the work now littering up the ground about the great canal will soon grow harmonious order. The Power House in the beginning will be extended only to cover three generators and three sets of water wheels, and power created by these wheels will be used to operate the channeling machines and the hoisting machinery which will be required to continue the excavation of the wheel pit for the receipt of the additional wheels and generators; also to continue the driving of the tunnel beyond the 7,000 ft. station to those points where other wheels may be required, either for additional electric power or for operating separate wheels under the control of manufacturers who rent them. The initial plant representing 15,000 horse power in the Power House and 3,000 horse power at the paper mill will be but part of the early installation. Groups of wheels arranged in sets of five to each pit will be arranged to give power in blocks of 1,000 horse power to a single manufactory, or blocks of less amounts to establishments that will have one wheel in common with two or more. This will suit the wants of manufacturers who desire to control in a measure their own power and to use it directly from the wheels without the intervention of electricity, compressed air or other modes of transmission. In all cases, however, where power less than 500 horse will be wanted, the electrical transmission will be resorted to.

One of the most striking uses of electricity will be exemplified in the great metallurgical works which will be erected on the bank of the river more than a mile away from the central station. In this establishment electricity will be used as a motive power and also for direct application to metallurgical processes, and though the power required would be more than sufficient to warrant the use of wheels devoted wholly to this purpose and controlled by the operators, preference has been given to the transmitted power on account of its exceeding convenience. It is worthy of note that at the present time many of the large establishments, both in this country and in Europe, are recognizing the advisability of creating their power at one locality where fuel can be handled cheaply and water for condensation obtained in abundance, the distribution of this power being entirely by electricity and the use of motors scattered about the establishment wherever required. Every great manufacturing establishment that has attempted this mode of operation has not only continued it, but from a small beginning has increased the electrical plant, as offering great advantages and convenience, as well as economy.

A junction railroad six miles in length has been constructed through the company's lands to enable all the main railroad lines passing Niagara Falls to deliver freight or to take goods from the factories to be established there. At present steam locomotives are used on the Junction road, but in the near future it is expected that it will be operated by electricity from the central power station.

The municipal water works that supply the City of

Niagara Falls, including the lands to be improved by the Niagara Falls Power Co., and also by a development company, have been removed from their old lo-

DISCHARGE PORTAL.

cation at the basin of the hydraulic canal to a point nearer to the new canal above the rapids and will eventually be transferred to a point still higher up the river where the best water can be obtained. The pumping is at present done by steam and will be until electricity can be furnished from the Power station.

A very complete trolley road has been established to carry passengers to and from the Falls and to all points of the City of Niagara Falls. Many convenient dwelling houses have been erected by the land improvement companies, and factories are to be built of convenient size, each capable of extension as the demands of the tenants call for additional room. This feature of the enterprise will make Niagara Falls attractive to manufacturers on account of the cheap power and reasonable rent, with no possible geographical objection to the location for any of the industries that can flourish in the Northern States. Proximity to the British possessions, as well as nearness to the home markets by rail and by water, with cheap power, is attractive, and abundance of labor will flock to a locality that has all the advantages incident to one of the wonders of the world and climatic conditions that are exceptional for the invigorating healthfulness of the air.

Bulletin No. 34, issued Feb. 26th, 1891, by the Census Bureau, gives information of importance in reference to the position occupied by Niagara Falls in relation to the population of the country. It must be borne in mind that the whole area of the United States, considered as a plane of no weight, has its centre of area somewheres in Kansas, but the centre of population lies to the west of Niagara Falls, latitude 39° 11′ 56″, longitude 85° 32′ 53″, in the southern part of Indiana, a little west and south of Greensburgh, the county seat of Decatur Co., and twenty miles east of Columbus, Ind. This centre of population has, in advancing westward since 1799, deviated but little in parallel of latitude, oscillating slightly on either side of latitude 39, but proceeding westward at an average rate of about 50 miles in each decade, sometimes less and sometimes more, as between 1850 and 1860, when the jump was 81 miles, caused by the sudden accession of population to the Pacific Coast. Niagara Falls falling to the east of the centre of population, bears a relation to the number of inhabitants in two important particulars, first as its being close to the densest population, and second, being so situated as to have remarkable advantages in railroad and water communication by canal, by the lakes, and by all the great trunk lines of railroads that run east and west.

The important consideration in estimating the value of this stupendous water power is its ability to distribute that power where it can be used to the best advantage beyond the local development at Niagara Falls itself. It is absolutely certain, from what has already been done elsewhere, that profitable transmission to a distance of 150 miles is only within the existing practice of distributed power. This 150 miles from Niagara Falls in a straight line brings us to within ninety miles of the city of New York, and if we assume as probable economical transmission to a distance of 320 miles, we have an area, including the densest population, taking in Columbus, Ohio, touching Washington, D. C., including Philadelphia and New York, and the whole of the states of Pennsylvania, New York, part of Maryland, the northern part of Virginia and West Virginia, more than two-thirds of Ohio, fully three-quarters of Michigan, beside reaching to Montreal in Canada, thus showing that the situation of Niagara Falls is phenomenal in its ability to distribute the power over an area that furnishes the most desirable market for its profitable development. If in the near future Chicago can receive its power from Niagara, then the whole of New England, with the exception of Maine, will come within reach of the Falls. Is it possible to conceive of a location more nearly central to the densest population and the greatest need for distributed power than the location fixed by nature for this development? Niagara Falls would still be the great Falls of the world with a distribution of power more than equal to all that the coal mines of Pennsylvania can supply.

Wind and water form the two natural sources of power. Water when used with water wheels yields its power solely from gravity, and yet, all things considered, it is the most economical source of energy. Water power alone without some economic mode of transmitting its energy has, however, the disadvantage of being fixed as to location. As compared to coal it is not transportable. Coal mined in Pennsylvannia can be used for power in any locality, the cost of power created by the combustion of coal being influenced only by the first cost of the fuel and its added cost of transportation. Each pound of coal burned can yield only some fraction of its total heat value as power, and when so used, so far as we know, there seems to be no tendency in nature to restore the coal that has been burned. Water cannot be transported as coal can. The value of a water fall being measured by its head, its quantity and its uniformity represents the force of gravity only. In using water for power we are using the constantly acting attraction of gravitation. A reliable, uniform water supply, such as is ideally represented at Niagara Falls, is the nearest obtainable approach to perpetual motion.

The water yielding its power by gravity at Niagara Falls, speeds away to the ocean, where it is vaporized and passes inland to be deposited on the rainshed that inclines towards the Great Lakes that feed Niagara Falls. Niagara Falls owes its power to the orderly operation of the laws that govern the Universe. The immense size of the lake reservoirs and the volume of water stored in them above Niagara Falls, insure conditions of stability. That the Niagara River does not vary materially from day to day is on account of the enormous area drained and the varying climatic conditions that effect the condensation of the vapor passing inland from the ocean. The water from a portion of Canada flows down to the lake and each of all the watersheds that tend towards the lakes delivers the rainfall by rivers and streams that flow into these lakes. A small impounded mass of water seldom represents a uniform water power, as it is likely to be affected by drought or suddenly increased by floods, both conditions detrimental to the stream as a source of power. Over such an area as is represented by the watershed of the Great Lakes these varying climatic conditions average themselves, and the rise and fall of the water in the lakes is less noticeable on account of the area covered, just as the ocean seems not to vary except by the tidal disturbances, so is the steadiness of the flow from Lake Erie to Niagara Falls seemingly uniform, warranting unusual care to insure uninterupted transmission of the power to those who will in the future demand their share of this great natural souce of power now for the first time to extend beyond a local use.

The Hydraulic Canal.

BY W. C. JOHNSON, C. E.

AS the waters of the Niagara River pass down through the Rapids and over the Falls they make a descent of about two hundred and fourteen feet in a distance of less than a mile. A force is thus generated equal to several millions of horse-power.

One of the things that most naturally occurs to the thinking man is the possibilities of the employment of this energy in useful work.

The simplest means of utilizing this force in a small way was by cutting canals along the river by the rapids above the Falls and discharging again into the river at a point a little distance below the intake.

So it has happened that from the earliest times mills were built at various points along the rapids above the Falls. The first use of the power appears to have been for a saw-mill which was erected about 1725, to supply lumber for the use of Fort Niagara, and from time to time until the lands along the rapids were taken by the State of New York for a Reservation, mills of various sorts were built and supplied with power from this source.

Only a small amount of power could be obtained in this way, and the building of mills in close proximity to the Falls was objectionable.

In 1847 Augustus Porter outlined the plan on which the present Hydraulic canal is built.

The circular issued by him at that time was accompanied by a map showing the canal very much as it stands to-day.

In 1842 negotiations were commenced with Caleb J. Woodhull and Walter Bryant, and an agreement was finally reached with these gentlemen by which they were to construct a canal and were to receive a right of way one hundred feet wide for this canal and a certain amount of land at its terminus. Ground was broken by them in 1853, and the work was carried on for about sixteen months. It was then suspended for lack of funds, and nothing more was done until 1858 when Stephen N. Allen took up the work and carried it forward for a time. After that, Horace H. Day took up the matter, and in 1861 completed a canal about thirty-five feet in width and about eight feet deep.

The location of the entrance to this canal was most wisely chosen. Just before the river commences its rapid descent to the brink of the Falls, the last of the small islands have been passed and it stretches out calm and deep, and more than a mile in width.

From this point the canal extends in the most

direct line to the edge of the high bluff below the Falls and by traversing a distance of forty-four hundred feet reaches a point where its water stands two hundred and fourteen feet above the water in the river below.

Great as were the evident advantages of this canal as a source of power it happened, from various causes, that no mills were built to use the water from it until 1870, when Mr. C. B. Gaskill built a small grist mill on the site of his present large and modern flouring mill.

In 1875 the canal and all its appurtanences were purchased by Mr. Jacob F. Schoellkopf of Buffalo, who organized the Niagara Falls Hydraulic Power and Manufacturing Company, of which he is still the president.

Since that time the building of mills upon its banks has gone steadily forward until there are at present fourteen large water wheels supplied with water from the canal, and the mills which they operate turn out about four thousand barrels of flour, and forty tons of paper every day, besides much other minor products and directly or indirectly afford employment for a large percentage of the population of the city of Niagara Falls.

By the terms of the grant to the builders of this canal the land was conveyed to them only to the edge of the high bank, and the sloping bank below still remained in the hands of the original owners.

This permitted the use of only about one-half the available head, but this mattered little at that time, as no water-wheel maker would have dared to put his wheel under a head of more than one hundred feet. Many were the failures of wheels in trying to use the hitherto unprecedented head of one hundred feet. All these difficulties have been overcome however.

The title to the bank below has been acquired by the company owning the canal, and during the past year a large wood pulp mill has been built by the water's edge below the high bank, taking its supply from the water which has heretofore been wasted from the mill above. The wheel which operates this mill is sixty inches in diameter, works under a head of one hundred and twenty-five feet, and is probably developing more power than any other single wheel in the world.

The growth of the manufacturing industries at this point has been such as to very nearly exhaust the power of the canal as originally built by Mr. Day. With a view to providing themselves with a supply of power for future demands, the company, about a year ago, commenced an enlargement of the canal to a little more than double its original capacity.

The enlargement now in progress is expected to be completed by the coming autumn, and will provide about thirty thousand horse-power.

The right of way occupied by the Hydraulic Canal

is one hundred feet in width, and it is the intention of the owners to enlarge the canal until it occupies the entire right of way, and to deepen it sufficiently to supply on the aggregate about one hundred thousand horse-power.

Power will, in the future, doubtless be developed by using the water under the full head of two hundred and fourteen feet.

The bank of the river for about a mile below the present mills is owned by the company, and affords excellent sites for mills requiring large amounts of power.

In addition to supplying power to these mills the lower bank offers a most excellent chance for the development of power to be transmitted to a distance by electricity or other means.

For this latter purpose no more favorable place could well be imagined.

A large volume of water is available where it can be used under a head of more than two hundred feet, and the wheels can be so placed that the generators can be belted directly to them without the intervention of long and cumbersome shafts or drives.

In power already developed and in possibilities of further development the plant of the Niagara Falls Hydraulic Power and Manufacturing Company deserves to rank among the first of the great water powers of the world.

www.ingramcontent.com/pod-product-compliance
Lightning Source LLC
Chambersburg PA
CBHW031739230426
43669CB00007B/401